ELISABETH

ELISABETH

Little Sister of the Poor

1902-1948

**Written by a
Little Sister of the Poor**

**Translated from the French
by the
Little Sisters of the Poor**

Contents

Preface

You have asked me to write my memories of
Sister Elisabeth. I am not among those who were
very close to her during life, either in family —
as were her brothers and sisters, or in her religious
vocation — as were her Superiors, her Sisters, her
Novices, and the Aged for whom she cared. However, in the few visits she made to Mongré, I was
deeply impressed by her superiority on a human
level which far exceeded that of most other girls
whom God sent my way. In what did such superiority consist? It would be difficult to analyse. In
a word, it is a light, like a ray of sunshine giving
brilliance to the countryside, which makes one say,
"Now, there is a person of great worth." Experience has shown that hardly two persons out of ten
ever rise much above the common level, giving

hope for great achievements in the future. Miss Elisabeth Louisgrand immediately impressed me; and so deeply that, whether or not she would ever become a religious, it seemed to me that, gifted as she was by Providence, she would lead an exemplary and fruitful life. Nothing about her ever lessened my conviction that she was an exceptionally gifted person.

She did not know for what task God was preparing her by these gifts. Her keen intelligence would have enabled her to undertake any career, no matter how difficult. Her strong will made her capable of sustained effort; her considerate feelings for others won her the friendship of the finest and most cultivated persons; a buoyant and almost constant cheerfulness gave to her open features and frank manner the charm of unalloyed goodness. Lastly, by shunning everything that was petty, commonplace or narrow-minded, her heart differed from those which do not know how to love unselfishly. It overflowed with generosity.

I am not making things up. I am simply describing the impression engraved on my mind.

When the question arose of choosing that way of life towards which Providence seemed to be leading her, she was neither hindered nor held back by the difficulties of an arduous undertaking. On the contrary, as though drawn by a magnet, she sought the path which led to the heights. To begin with, she dismissed whatever would not require effort— I would even say heroism—on her part. This simplified the choice of her future, for both heights and depths exercised a strong attraction over her, to which it was more difficult for her to resist than to yield. She was not one to banish the thought of a religious vocation through fear of sacrifice. To carry her cross after Jesus, immediately appeared to her as an ideal. I can vouch for the fact that, if she was ready to renounce a career in the world and give herself unreservedly to religious life, it was solely for the most unselfish motives and in the hope of sacrificing herself entirely in serving the poor.

Spiritual directors have no difficulty guiding souls in whom the Holy Spirit reveals His presence and His strength so clearly.

I can affirm—and perhaps I am the only one who can—that her decision to enter the Little Sisters of the Poor was taken in two steps. This chosen soul wanted, first of all, to become a religious solely through a motive of magnanimity, persuaded that she would thereby, in taking religious vows, be leading the most courageous and fruitful type of life. Then, after much consideration, she decided to enter the Congregation of the Little Sisters of the Poor because she was convinced that her dedication would, in that way, be unknown to the world and devoid of earthly reward. She feared the baseness of pride which can insinuate itself into virtue. She considered it more difficult to reach the pinnacle of sanctity in humility, than to do so in the sight of men and with the certainty of winning their esteem.

I can vouch for this by a testimony which until now has been kept confidential.

Once she became a religious, she lived under the influence of the Holy Spirit. Her director no longer knew anything about the graces God was granting *her. Nor could her family suspect her spiritual ascent. Fortunately, some features of her spiritual profile have been gathered from her functions as Novice Mistress. I have just read her biography. It is a study and it is beautiful. I would like to go back over every page of these memories, to affirm that I can truly recognize her, and that she was really like that. Nothing related there astonishes me. Things came about as they did because she was destined to rise to such perfection.*

To avoid multiplying praise after reading a life of such supernatural beauty, I shall limit myself to making just one observation.

The authentic sign of highest sanctity is purity of love. For a long time, souls can imagine that their love of God is very pure. Then, after much experience, they finally see that their love badly needed to be purified. But it could only be purified by the Holy Spirit and by an utter emptying of self. The merely human is mingled in the whole spiritual life, like cockle among the wheat, and when the human is excessively rich it risks absorbing, to its own advantage, a good part of what is gained by a virtuous life. It seems to me that Sister Elisabeth very soon understood the necessity of an active and passive purification, and laboured with admirable success to lose herself completely in the Trinity.

Her words and her writings are like crystal in the sunshine. It can clearly be seen that God's Will alone reigned in this soul which suffered so much. His presence was her sole interest, and enlightened her on all occasions. In her charity towards her neighbor, God's love alone occupied her heart. Beyond all things on the horizon of her universe, she perceived the Trinity. Only the hope of soon beholding this holy and adorable Trinity sustained her ardour. The thirst for perfection which had become a thirst for God, then a thirst for love and for the Beatitude of the Father, Son and Holy Spirit, burned within her ardent soul. This is probably the reason why Sister Elisabeth, who could still have done so much good on earth, died young, while her life was yet in full bloom. To her prayerful supplication, "Veni Domine Jesu', the heavenly Bridegroom replied, "Veni".

It is not the length of life that God takes into consideration when He calls His Saints to Paradise. It is not to impoverish the Church Militant or the Congregation where He had placed them. By their power in Heaven, they become much more valuable, active, and of benefit to the souls confided to them than they would have been during their earthly lives. Those who feel deprived of Sister Elisabeth's visible presence must surely abound in this sure consolation. The Little Sisters of the Poor have another protectress in heaven.

Fr. Charmot, S.J.
Instructor of Tertianship

Paray, November 19, 1953
Feast of St. Elizabeth

"We will never realise how much we owe our parents."

Family Life

Evenings were spent around the family table, beneath the light of the hanging brass lamp.

In the evening, when all was quiet, the children would study their lessons for the next day and their parents, facing one another, would read. Each one spontaneously taking, for any family gathering, the usual place he or she occupied at meal-times.

When the day's accounts were done, Mr. Louis-grand glanced through the newspaper, at times reading aloud an interesting article or news item. Opinions and impressions were voiced, and the discussion became lively. All were of one mind and heart. How good it was to be together! It was the time to talk things over . . .

Babeth at four years of age.

When nine o'clock struck, there was a sharp little knock on the table. Books were closed, not without a few sighs! Then the head of the family began night prayer. On their knees, their hands joined, the others replied . . .

Such was the warm atmosphere of home, where close family life thrived. Strong convictions maintained the spiritual climate.

Mr. Louisgrand had great devotion to the Sacred Heart, the Friend of the family, solemnly enthroned in the home. He had taken the children, big and small alike, to Paray-le-Monial several times. Priority was given to spiritual values, and his personality was governed by the "consciousness of God". Even before any of them considered religious life, he had already declared that he would "give 50% of his children to God if that was what God asked of him". God took him at his word, and his offer became a reality. The eldest son, on the day of his Ordination, expressed his gratitude by having printed, on his commemorative cards: "Filii sanctorum sumus".

Although there was great openness to others, the central focus was on the family. It revolved around the personality of Mr. Louisgrand. Ever at his side, his devoted wife would constantly put herself aside to uphold the father's authority, without ever supplanting it.

She was a valiant, humble woman, and the living soul of the family to which she had given four boys and four girls, as well as a set of twins who died in infancy.

For both the younger and the older children, "our Parents" symbolised home—its soul, its spirit, its heart, its life, its vibrant and loving closeness. This frequently used expression summarised their respectful admiration and attachment to a treasure shared in common. Babeth often repeated, "We will never realise how much we owe our Parents."

☐

Elisabeth, affectionately called Babeth in family, was a blue-eyed adolescent, with her hair rolled up in a thick bun on the back of her neck.

Vigour and determination—dominant traits of her personality—were reflected even in her appearance. She gave the impression of being well-balanced. It was all the more striking to those who had known her as a child and remembered her as a frail, timid and overly sensitive little girl, whose blond hair, unruly despite her mother's care, fell to her shoulders, and whose clear, smiling blue eyes shone brightly from beneath her slightly slanted brows.

What precious memories Babeth had of her childhood! Neulize . . . the village deep in the woods, the big house with its immense grounds—a real earthly paradise which belonged to them. The "old path" leading to the tiny Calvary chapel, the armfuls of primroses brought home from country walks in springtime to decorate Saint Joseph's statue in the hallway.

Together with her elder sister Germaine, and Robert who followed her closely, Elisabeth was one of the three "oldest". The expression implicitly carried with it a host of enviable privileges, which were consequently admired and sought after by the "band of little ones".

For Babeth, Neulize was especially connected with the memory of her First Holy Communion, on April 2nd 1911, and of her first call. Returning home, she related how Jesus wanted her for Himself and, in her emotion, she broke into tears. Germaine was astonished: Jesus had not asked her for anything. Why was Babeth crying?

That same year the family left their country home and moved to Villefranche. There the boys could go to the Jesuit College at Mongré. The girls could be day pupils at the Ursuline school, and afterwards attend the boarding school at the Benedictine Monastery of Pradines.

At school, Babeth soon became outstanding. She had a lively imagination and shared her ideas, discussing them with her friends. The timid little girl was proving to be determined, highly endowed, and anxious to develop her potential to the fullest. Half-measures were unknown to her. Whenever she undertook anything, she had to carry it out to the very end, no matter what the cost.

At twenty, Babeth was said to be "imposing". She was so, in fact, by that remarkably profound "something", which she retained all her life. Although not very gifted for housework, she did not disdain it. Housekeeping occupied her mornings. When it was her week in the kitchen, there were always surprises — original recipes, cakes, clever decorations — and the mayonnaise sauces she made were famous.

When springtime came, Mrs. Louisgrand and the little ones would go to Collonges, the country house on the banks of the Saône. Germaine and Babeth would stay in Villefranche with their father. Babeth just loved that!

"Actually, what God loves is heroism."
Du Plessis de Grenedan

How I Love Life!

How often Babeth said this, and it was true. She enjoyed everything—the deep joys of close family life, the gladness of friendship, the beauties of literature and music.

"Back home, we might have to sing for our supper . . . but I'll play Chopin's waltzes for you."

Beethoven and Chopin were her favorite composers. While playing "L'Appassionata", the tempo was so lively that her bun sometimes fell loose.

Unforgettable, those midnight Masses in the Chapel of Our Lady at Mongré. For days afterwards, she would be humming the familiar carols and organ preludes.

Sensitive to the beauties of nature, she would stroll along the paths in the grounds, especially the one lined with chestnut trees and which resembled a beautiful Gothic vault, reflecting the while on the conference she had just heard. In passing, she would admire a certain scene, a play of light, a harmony of colours.

She read extensively — basic works, anything solid that appeared: Bourget, Peguy . . . Rostand, whose keen sense of humour delighted her.

Her youthful enthusiasm was contagious and spread beyond the confines of her family, making her the centre of attraction among her friends. She was outstanding for her intellectual qualities and for her keen mind, direct and accurate, enabling her to quickly grasp the different sides of an issue in its most subtle aspects, and capable of easily and correctly assimilating them.

In a close-knit circle of friends called "the group", discussions were lively. When "Paroles d'un Revenant" appeared, Babeth worked with tremendous enthusiasm to set forth its underlying principles. Page by page, she annotated the entire volume.

☐

At home, she was called "Monsignor". No need to say more!

Her interference in everything was willingly accepted; her spontaneousness, her innate goodness, her thoughtful, affectionate love for her family, made what at times seem like "domination" be quickly forgotten. Others readily asked her advice, only to discover afterwards that, once given, it was in reality more like a strict and detailed command.

Even her own father did not hesitate to tell her his plans for Lent, submitting them to her judgment. "Monsignor" carried out her functions in great simplicity, yet not without somewhat imposing her own way.

She would decide every question, even going so far as to advise one of those under her "direction" against making a general confession!

Her precocious maturity of judgment was accompanied by a real spontaneity. It was Babeth who put life into family festivities!

September 22nd, her father's name-day gave a solemn tone to the end of vacation. There was usually a play of some sort, and a gymnastic competition. The theatrical part was Babeth's domain. She took charge of rehearsals, and of making sure everyone memorized their roles. Oh, those rehearsals!

At times, Babeth's gaiety was somewhat out of place—her fits of laughter were legendary. Having her along for certain visits or when receiving company could really be tormenting, for she had a "really French" mentality, and immediately saw the funny side of people and of things.

Never, for anything in the world, would Babeth have wanted to hurt anyone. Her tactfulness would not allow teasing to degenerate into ridicule. Years after she had left home, one of the old sewing maids—rather shy and not given to expressing her gratitude — exclaimed spontaneously, "How kind Miss Elisabeth was!"

The younger ones knew this better than anyone

else. On the opening day of school, the boys would proudly show off their new books and notebooks, with headings and titles perfectly written on the covers. Looking over their shoulders, the lads next to them would whisper admiringly, "What fancy writing! Did you do that?"

"Me? No. My sister did . . ."

Handwriting was not Babeth's only speciality. In "delicate" situations, she was a first-class one to turn to: whenever a misdemeanour brought on the possibility of a general punishment, Babeth would take the blame. When anyone was sick, she would give up her meetings and outings to stay at home with them.

□

There was nothing commonplace about Babeth. In everything, she dwelt on a higher level, where her richly endowed personality quite naturally placed her.

She tried to tune to her own wavelength those with whom she came in contact. The intellectual formation of her brothers and sisters preoccupied her, but their spiritual formation concerned her even more. She prepared them herself for their First Holy Communion, trying to make them correspond personally, to communicate her own enthusiasm, her determination to choose what cost the most—the sure way of sacrifice. If Marie-Thérèse and Andrée listened quietly, almost indifferently, to the reading of the Passion, Babeth would become indignant at their passive attitude. "I just cannot understand how a young Christian can listen to the story of Our Lord's sufferings without shedding a tear!" The exclamation was not ineffective—at

once, her listeners broke into heart-rending sobs
. . . Bible history, when told by Babeth, became
alive and interesting. Peter, the youngest, who was
her godchild, would listen fascinated, small though
he was.

Often, as she read a book, Babeth would jot
down a thought which struck her, mark certain
lines, and then share her findings with you:

> "To acquire moral beauty, to radiate it, is to
> become an apostle, even without a given field
> of action, simply by the beauty of one's life."
>
> Mgr. Tissier.
>
> "Actually, what God loves is heroism. All
> His friends, sooner or later, pass through
> trials and are given the grace to become heros."
>
> Du Plessis de Grenedan.

From the time she was seventeen, Babeth used
to speak openly about her religious vocation. Her
lively cheerfulness was misleading for those who
only met her occasionally at social gatherings, but
those close to her made no mistake about it.

Although she was attracted and captivated by
everything, it was God who held the strongest attraction for her. She already belonged so entirely to
Him that He could treat her as His very own, as
the object of His love. Being intransigent with
herself in everything, and all the more so on this
point, she had a very high ideal of religious life.
What she could not manage to define was how and
where she was to fulfil this ideal. Each new experience in her contacts with different religious
Congregations only increased her interior turmoil.

Wavering, anxious, searching, she could find no rest, her soul sad to the point of desolation. How mysterious is such suffering in a soul tormented by Love and not knowing how to respond to it. The gentleness and sureness of God's plan escaped her. It would be discovered only later—exceedingly rich and captivating—in the perspective of the past. So painful at the time however, that she would one day admit, "It sometimes happens that even years later, our trials are as burdensome and as present to us as they were at the time they occurred."

Her family was concerned about not always being able to understand her. There were Holy Hours in the "girls' room" in the evenings, and pilgrimages to Ars for the four of them. It was pleasant, walking in the fresh morning air, crossing the Saône at the old Jassans Bridge, and following paths bordered with poplars and small cottages, to arrive in the little village nestling on the plain. They would receive Communion in the old church adjoining the basilica, pray before the shrine where the body of the saint lay intact, then visit the old presbytery. All the souvenirs of the humble Curé of Ars were there: his Mass vestments, his instruments of penance, his wooden bed burned by the "grappin" and, in the fireplace, near a bowl, an old frying-pan — the extent of Monsieur Vianney's kitchen utensils.

As the sun rose higher in the sky, the four girls would find a grassy spot in the shade, and picnic before starting for home. Somehow the walk back always seemed longer than twelve kilometers.

On those evenings, Babeth would feel a little

peace invade her soul . . .

□

She would be twenty-three on July 6th 1925. One April afternoon, she went for a walk with her father. Suddenly, a cloudburst drenched the countryside, the "Chemin des Rousses" became a small river, and the nearby Home of the Little Sisters of the Poor was the only place they could find to take shelter.

The Little Sisters were not unknown to them. The collecting Sisters came regularly to the pharmacy, and would go up to the first floor to see Mrs. Louisgrand. Babeth never went to the parlour when they came: "Those nuns don't interest me!"

Mr. Louisgrand rang the doorbell and they hastened into the small reception area to wait for the rain to stop. When the sky cleared, her father thanked the Sister, and the two of them left. Apart from a few polite words, not much had been said. Nevertheless, Babeth seemed thoughtful, and startled her sister by exclaiming, "The Little Sisters . . . after all, why not? . . . I would never have given them a thought!"

Was that where God wanted her? When she asked the experienced counsellor who knew her well, he suggested that she give it some consideration. He who was so anxious to see Elisabeth's state of incertitude come to an end, had never thought such a step possible. Quickly, however, with his supernatural judgment he discerned the reality of a true calling and, from then on, not only did he give his consent, but also encouraged her.

Miss Elisabeth Louisgrand at twenty-three
years of age.

Babeth sensed that she would have to sacrifice absolutely everything, but she was at peace. She had struggled for so long, and her expectations had so often been disappointed. To "make sure", she went back alone to the "Chemin des Rousses." The conversation was brief. She expressed her desire for religious life in which she could give herself entirely, inquired about the life of the Little Sisters and about their apostolate. She spoke with composure, decidely; nothing led to suspect her great anxiety of soul. When she returned home, she was beaming.

"Well?"

"Well, I think I've found the right one this time!"

Her aspirations, desires, ideals — all were blended harmoniously in this answer God had just given her. She knew now that it was there that she would find Him, without any danger of illusion, in humility.

□

The vacation of 1925 was to be her last. At Mount d'Or and Mount Cindre, there was no end to long hikes and bicycling. Nothing tired Babeth. More than ever, she was expansive and exuberant. They talked for hours on end about everything under the sun. Mr. and Mrs. Louisgrand smiled approvingly at the earnestness of their reflections.

Each year, October meant the re-opening of school, and as soon as they returned to Villefranche, the family was dispersed. Separations were so much a part of this month, that leaving home could not take place at any other time. So Babeth chose to leave on the 7th.

To all appearances, it was a day like any other. As she had so often done before, Babeth set off, together with her mother and father. This time, however, as she neared the bend in the road, she stopped, turned around, and took a last look at home—at the warm seedbed where God had nurtured her. A second later, her slim figure was out of sight. Collonges would never see her again.

Two days later, she was writing from Lyons, where she had gone as an aspirant.

"What a day it was, last Tuesday! I'm still shattered, exhausted, and yet I've already found some compensation. The elderly ladies are so kind—not to mention the Little Sisters! And then too, my dear Parents, you have understood my vocation of Little Sister. How good it is to be more united than ever, and to offer our great sacrifice together."

Towards her family, Babeth was putting on a brave front. In reality, the first weeks were difficult ones. At times, it was hard—very hard. The "Master" was leaving her in darkness, and she felt very much alone. This affected everything, and her health began to suffer to such an extent as to cause some concern.

Towards the end of February, there was a definite change for the better in this regard. She had said nothing to anyone about her moral lassitude, and no one was aware of it. The "Master" knew, and that was sufficient. One day, when she was battling against discouragement and the longing to go home, God sent her a little ray of light in quite a strange manner. She was at the bedside of a sick lady, who seemed to be unconscious. All of a sudden she sat up, looked straight at Babeth, and murmured, "Sister . . . don't leave . . . You'd regret it the rest of your life." Then she fell back on her pillows.

Babeth believed she was doing what God wanted of her. What further reassurance did she need to keep going?

She was due to leave for the novitiate at the end of March, and wrote to tell her family.

"I shall be leaving on March 22nd, so you are invited to come for a visit and have dinner with me. Although we shall have to say good-bye, I am sure it will be a happy day. It will be hard for you, I know, and I am asking God to make your sacrifice easier. . . . It seems that La Tour is simply beautiful in the spring!"

"We belong to a God who was annihilated, humiliated, and it is from those who espouse His lowly condition and His sufferings that He receives genuine praise."

The 'All' of God.

"It seems that La Tour is simply beautiful in the spring. . . ." Elisabeth did not see any of its beauty the first evening, for night had already fallen over the old monastic dwelling when she arrived. The following morning began with the reception of a new name. Babeth would be keeping her baptismal name, signifying intimacy with God, and adding to it "Gabriel"—"strength of God".

"I am now Little Sister Elisabeth de Saint-Gabriel. What do you think of that? You will be pleased with my new name, won't you? . . . You cannot imagine how beautiful La Tour is—the little I have seen just thrills me. It is immense,

immense . . . such sweeping horizons, with woods
and fields as far as the eye can see. The chapel is
magnificent, a real little church, filled with the
black capes of the novices. Do pray hard, so that
I will make a fervent novitiate. . . ."

Babeth was moved to the very depths of her
soul. The exclamation marks and suspension dots
in her letters betrayed her inability to describe
things, and superlative adjectives abounded. Her
eagerness was apparent in everything. She was
"ardent, even-tempered, laughing easily! . . . enthusiastic and full of life." Once a group of novices
was voicing impressions about the cape worn by
the Little Sisters. In the past, its hood billowing
in the wind had not always won unanimous favour.
"I found it fascinating", enjoined Sister Elisabeth.

When writing home, she described La Tour.
"The novitiate grounds are splendid, with beautiful trees—cedars, pines, chestnuts . . . I am enjoy-
ing this lovely springtime immensely. Primroses
and violets form a real carpet (a rather stereo-
typed expression! . . . but never mind!) I'm
equipped with a pair of enormous wooden shoes
for outdoors, and am now becoming quite nimble
on my feet wearing them, but it wasn't easy to
begin with. . . . You should see me in my outfit!"

"The further I go, the more I appreciate the
Congregation, and the more I thank God. . . . It is
one huge family to which I am becoming pas-
sionately attached, without that lessening in any
way my love for my first family—at all, at all!
. . . I am overwhelmed with graces. Everything
here leads to detachment; charity reigns in a mar-
vellous way, and that is what makes us find God."

In all this spirited chatter, some phrases stand out: "Everything here leads to detachment . . . find God." When, later on, she would say that "suffering is the best novitiate", she would be summing up her own.

The sacrifice came neither from without, nor from her sisters, nor from her formation. Besides, the discipline in her family upbringing rather prepared her for community life and its regular observances. Her suffering came from God. Her "Master", her "Great Master", as she already loved to call Him, had taken possession of her soul. He was going to bring about a complete reversal of values. She knew moments of anguish, painful perplexity, entire periods of complete disorientation, anxiety and scruples.

The feast of Saint Michael was the day set for the reception of the Holy Habit. She did not draw back from her offering — everything had been accepted beforehand. "Blessed are those who accept everything without understanding", she would write.

"There is a joy which, according to Our Lord's words, 'no one can take from us.' It is the joy found in the generous gift of self, in attentive, loving fidelity, and in sacrifice accepted and sought after."

"Since I have become a novice, I seem to understand a little better each day what a grace the life of a Little Sister is. Here too, our love for the Poor grows. All those "elderly folk" the world over, whom we shall lead to heaven. What a wonderful thought!"

Over and over, she repeated in her letters, "Pray for me, so that I will love Our Lord ardently!"

Love Him ardently, truly, genuinely, profoundly—
how frequently these expressions are to be found,
often underlined or within quotation marks:

"Above all, love Our Lord, love Him 'genuinely'.
Not only when all is going well, but all the more
so in moments of sacrifice and repugnance. Love
Him with a strong, genuine love, nourished by
fidelity and sacrifice. Pray with all your heart, not
seeking consolation but rather the strength to love,
to love realistically. . . . Time does not matter to
God, for He is eternal. Love alone matters to Him.
We do not love Him enough, we do not seek Him
with the ardent desire, that 'thirst' which burned
in the hearts of the saints. We must ask the Holy
Spirit to make us understand our religious life, its
exigencies, so as to live it not just as good, 'pious
women', but as saints. In our hearts, the Name of
Jesus must be written in place of 'me'."

Already at that period of her life, she had understood that it is impossible to separate love from
suffering:

"It is impossible to become a saint without
suffering. A loving heart yearns to share everything with the Beloved . . . 'He' is all, He is all
powerful. He alone has the right to ask great
sacrifices, because while asking, He gives to the
soul who abandons herself generously to Him."

This was her own attitude. During her novitiate,
God was Master, and He Himself fashioned her,
revealing the mystery of His humility, His abase-
ment, His solitude and suffering. This was "her"
grace. She was never to cease contemplating it,
sounding its depths, exploiting its treasures:

"We belong to a God who was annihilated,

humiliated, and it is from those who espouse His lowly condition and His sufferings that He receives genuine praise. . . . After all, becoming one with Him is not something to take lightly."

She sought to understand better the value of God's gift:

"If you only knew how wonderful it is to be a Little Sister! One really has to be holy to realise what a great grace it is, and to correspond with it. . . . My religious life is something so great for me. I haven't the right to live it half-heartedly. Every minute of it is given to me to unite me more intimately with God."

In the middle of February, 1928, she announced in her letter to Villefranche, "I shall be going on retreat on February 28th, and am counting very much on the help of your prayers."

What a great family event—Babeth's profession! "How we were all looking forward to it, and what a pleasant, warm family reunion it was", wrote her sister. "We were all so glad to see our Elisabeth again, so serenely happy and radiant."

In the depths of her soul, where her sensitivity had no access, all was at peace:

"The joy my first profession brings me, this deep inner happiness, must last throughout my entire religious life. If, unfortunately, it should disappear or diminish, I know that it would be my own fault, not God's. It would come from my lack of generosity, from giving in to myself, from laxity."

☐

She took with her to Bordeaux her happiness

and her desire to love ardently. Villefranche heard of it: ". . . We must, at all costs, climb together, each one at the pace God chooses."

For the time being, she accompanied on the collecting rounds, and made her ascent . . . on level ground. Her descriptions of the Bordeaux countryside filled pages:

"The countryside is so pretty at this time. Bordeaux is surrounded with little villages; it is a very wooded area, with lots of pine trees, and bright sunshine . . ."

In the autumn, her letter home made mention of a setback in her health.

"I am no longer out on the highways. With the fatigue of the collecting rounds this summer, I am a bit tired. . . . Obedience obliges me to rest, so I am doing some sewing."

Her tone was light, but not her "tiredness". Fortunately, it was discovered and treated in time. When Sister Elisabeth resumed activity, it was in the service of the Aged.

"Lately I have been going a lot to the ladies' infirmary, and there I am in my element. A little lady called Adèle, frail and wasted by extreme poverty, was called to God on Mother's feastday. Miss Anais thoroughly enjoyed the 'wedding', as she called it."

"The other day, I went to visit a little old lady. It was a charming scene . . . Mrs. Boris lives down a blind alley which hardly deserves the name. One of her relatives brought us in. A spiral staircase led to a dark corridor, and in a small room, there was Mrs. Boris, a slight, grey-haired figure, hidden beneath a suspicious-looking cap. . . . There was an accumulation of everything imaginable. To our question: 'Would you like to come to our home?' the rebellious little lady protested, 'No. I want to keep my independence, and go to bed whenever I feel like it.' Finally, won over by Mother's coaxing, she uncovered a bowl containing something shapeless that was swimming in thick gravy and whispered confidentially, 'It's rabbit in a bit of gravy . . . not so dry that way.' "

Some time later, charged with the men's infirmary, she continued on the same note:

"What 'treasures' these grandfathers are! There are all types. One was from the country, whose dark eyes seem to take extravagant pleasure in everything they see. After having tried on several sweaters, he told me why he is difficult to please: 'I'll tell you frankly. It's not because I'm fat, but because I'm a bit plump . . .'

And Sanitasse! A quiet old gentleman whose overcoat is so huge that one can't see him without first seeing his coat. Early each morning, he greets me with, 'Good morning, Good Mother', I haven't the heart to put him right."

In her duties of hospitality, she found what she was seeking above all—the possibility of intimate union with God.

"More and more I experience what real devotion to duty should be, and what the task of a Little Sister is. It is such a wonderful one!

To be sure, like anything else, our active life has its difficulties. But in living its simple round of activities, one discovers also all the means it offers to go to God, and to be purified of selfishness.

In work, and in charity towards the poor, there

are those opportunities for renunciation which contemplative religious have in their lives—not to mention that which is hardest in our work, and which doesn't appear to be so at first glance. The daily activity of running an employment involves much renunciation: monotony, the need for restraint and self-control so as to avoid infringing upon the exercises of piety. All of that is good for us . . .

In spite of everything, I'm still pitifully engulfed in selfishness. It is hard work to leave oneself and to let Our Lord be Master, but my confidence knows no bounds.

Those around her noticed her supernatural influence on the Aged. Naturally gifted to succeed in everything, she excelled even more in her apostolic endeavours. At the time, there was an old man who had done a lot of tiling in the Home. His work was well done, and he was happy doing it. When, because of infirmity, he was confined to the infirmary, active as he had been . . . there were outbursts. For no reason at all, he would threaten others with his cane. Sister Elisabeth spoke to him . . . he would be so happy if he would offer God everything that aggravated him. The next time he was annoyed, up in the air went his cane once more. "Well Louis?" Sister Elisabeth prompted. The old man looked at her. "You're right, Sister. I promised God I would be patient."

September 1929 brought with it a separation she felt keenly:

"God is asking a sacrifice such as I have not had since leaving home. Our Mother Superior is leaving Bordeaux and is being called to La Tour . . .

I owe her so very much; through her I learned the real meaning of abnegation."

A year later, and another separation:

"I must tell you the big news of the day—my Obedience. I shall be leaving Bordeaux on the 27th for Paris, and from there I'll be going to Dieppe."

DIEPPE, OCTOBER 18TH.

"This Obedience has shown me how advantageous it is to be governed by God's Will. The change was very easy. I already feel as though I have been here for ages, and I love my life as a Little Sister just as I did in Bordeaux. However, I have unforgettable memories of my first Home. I learned many things there, and acquired a real understanding of my vocation . . .

Here I am once again with the elderly men. They are different from those in Bordeaux — good hearted Normands, still strong and robust. There are forty-five of them . . . I'm already very fond of them."

One of them, with the clear sightedness of the lowly, soon named her "our new contemplative Sister". He was not mistaken. Her life was becoming more and more simplified:

"Abnegation is at the base of everything, and this is where the absolute need of God's grace makes itself felt.

My health is perfect. I am very much at home, and happier than ever.

After Christmas, I left the old men and am now taking care of the ladies . . . I felt the change a bit, but not for long. Anyway, there is little time to think about it, and besides, we can serve God and give Him our love no matter where we are."

Several weeks later, the sacrifice He asked of her wounded her heart. One morning, she received the news of her father's death. She knew he had been ill, but her mother's letters were not alarming to the extent of letting her foresee the approaching separation. She kept silent about it, and was as cheerful as ever during the afternoon recreation. Nonetheless, her shock and sorrow were tremendously deep.

"I never thought, never realised that Papa was so ill . . ." and she grasped hold of the truths of faith:

"God is the Master, and He is Goodness itself. . . . It is comforting for us to believe this and to be convinced of it. Dearest Mama, we must keep our eyes fixed on heaven, and on the Cross of Christ. I am begging Him to strengthen all of you and to bring us closer to Him."

Later, she again wrote to console the family:

"I have just renewed with all my heart my vows as a Little Sister. It is to Papa that I owe this vocation which prevented me from seeing him again, and allowed me to offer this sacrifice for him. How I experience the peaceful certitude of a deeper union, one that is no less real. How heartening to think of Papa's devotion to the Sacred Heart, Who called him to Himself just as the novena ended . . . I never felt so strongly the depth of love in our family, and how it reaches its fulfilment in God's love."

In May 1932, her sister, who had entered the Congregation in 1930, was going to make her profession, and Sister Elisabeth went to La Tour for the ceremony. What must such a reunion have been like? The closeness of years past—only now there was something stronger, deeper, richer. Doubtless, everyone felt the absence of those who were missing, but trial had purified their love and drawn them closer to each other. Sister Elisabeth rejoiced in seeing her loved ones "ascending" thus. To them, she appeared to be tired, but courageous and so supernatural in everything.

She returned to Dieppe, but not for long, for soon she would be called back to La Tour for the Second Novitiate.

□

She had been looking forward to this step.

"The Lord is guiding me, I lack nothing. He has led me to still, life-giving waters. He has turned to Himself all the powers of my soul.

These words come to my mind quite naturally.

1. Nothing has been lacking to me so far.

Looking back over the past with gratitude: Christian upbringing. Fervent First Holy Communion. Sacrament of Penance. Vocation. First Novitiate. Graces. Lights. The Cross also.

2. Trust: nothing will be lacking to me in the future.

A fervent novitiate. This entails so much. There's enough there to satisfy the highest aspirations."

"I am very happy. Please pray that I correspond to this great grace. The more I advance, the more I love the Congregation. It is so simple, it is so beautiful, and leads us so surely to pure love of God. . . . It is that same life we live here, together with the supernatural work of the Second Novitiate

—deeper and more realistic."

She has left no writings which date from this period. A harmonious blend of maturity and cheerfulness made her remarkable: "When I met her again, she seemed to be more experienced, but as pleasant, thoughtful and smiling as ever—even more so, and full of joy, but a joy that was more tranquil. With her sense of humour, she saw the funny side of things, and would make me want to laugh too, even during the time of silence. Once at recreation, she said to me: 'I make you want to laugh too, and I'm sorry. If only we could remain serious.' " [1]

Her deep happiness was reflected in her letter to her mother announcing the date of her perpetual vows.

"I know that everyone at home shares the great happiness which is mine as the day of our final profession draws near. The ceremony is set for March 8th . . . it is such a pure and deep joy, much like that of an approaching First Communion. Then too, this joy has been growing during these quiet months of grace.

You realise too how serious it is: it is the decisive step forward, forever, which I have been longing to make. But it must also be a step forward in holiness and in the total gift of myself. . . . In a few weeks, I should be able to let you know what my Obedience is, and what will be happening afterwards."

---

[1] Testimony of one of her companions in the novitiate.

View of the Novitiate of La Tour Saint Joseph.

> *"Jesus, Supreme Offering, take
> whatever I do not know how to give
> You. . . . Keep me as a constant offer-
> ing to Yourself, to others for Your
> sake, always through love and for the
> glory of 'our Father'."*

An Open Invitation ...

The long-awaited letter arrived in Villefranche.
". . . Perhaps Mama is already getting excited?
Well, she can quieten down . . . with a rather mischievous pleasure, I am purposely drawing this
out! I shall not be crossing the ocean, nor will I
be needing a trunk or provisions for a journey—
not even a short ride on the train. . . . Obedience is
keeping me here in La Tour, with the Little Sister
novices.

A new period is now opening out before me, and
my life is being given a new direction. You understand, don't you? There will be new responsibili-
ties as well, so please keep me in your prayers.

Contact with souls is always serious, even in a secondary role."

Formation-Aide in the novitiate. . . . On hearing this, her tears fell. To one of the parting sisters, she whispered, "Pray for me, so that God will give me the grace to do His Will generously. How I envy you, returning to the elderly folk."

But she had no illusions.

"If God has called us to religious life, it is not for the services we would be so happy to render to our Congregation. . . . It is uniquely to give Him souls, by forgetting ourselves entirely and generously accepting His divine and impenetrable Will."

She had all the aptitudes necessary for this new charge. Her natural and supernatural gifts were going to "yield" plentifully. She was not a brilliant speaker, but her every word carried weight. Her conferences were clear, precise and doctrinal. She reviewed them, developed them, making them easy to assimilate.

She was reproached for her vivacity, for being somewhat severe, somewhat stiff—consequences of a strong-willed character. She possessed the defects of her qualities. Strict, and even austere with herself, Sister Elisabeth did not understand how anyone could "argue with God". What she did herself, she required of others.

"What is essential for me to understand," she wrote, "is the spirit of this task (the formation of the novices) and with God's grace, to accomplish it with genuine abnegation. . . . It is something beautiful, even in a secondary role, to see souls developing, souls who are thirsting for God and who are generously striving to find Him. . . . We have some wonderful examples of generosity that are edifying. Then too, being obliged to speak about the necessity of virtue brings me, willy nilly, out of my tepidity . . ."

In this quiet atmosphere of silence which spoke of God, Sister Elisabeth's soul found freedom, became pacified, refined. Her letters did not say everything. They could not have expressed it:

"We must be unemcumbered, stripped of everything when we go before God; stripped especially of whatever we could believe to be due to our own merits. . . . Our one desire: to succeed in finding Jesus within ourselves in that hidden dwelling place where only humble, detached souls can discover Him. To do so, let us be willing to pay the price. Never could the cost be too much.

The more we deprive ourselves, the quicker we grow and become established in peace. We must be generous, cost what it may . . . we must expect to suffer and be prepared for it. We have no idea what kind of purification God has in store for us. Love does not draw to itself, but rather gives of itself.

All our efforts in this poor world and each passing day, filled as they are with our imperfections, should result in tearing us away from ourselves, so that we may give ourselves unreservedly to Our Lord, to His love, to the search for Him alone. It takes repeated experiences and also suffering to advance in this domain."

In a letter written a year before her death, she described this work of detachment, such as she had practised it:

" . . . The further you go, the more you will

experience the profound joy of belonging to Our Lord, of having given our life to Him, and of wanting nothing but Him alone. As the years pass, the demands of a religious vocation become more apparent, more precise and absolute. Our Lord wants 'everything', and it is by this generous gift of everything that the soul responds to her vocation, fulfills God's plans and sanctifies herself.

It is very simple. We need only follow the light given each day, and accept the sacrifice of the present moment, or accomplish the duty at hand with love and fidelity. It is simple, yet at the same time difficult, because it requires continual attention on our part, and constant and docile generosity to obey the inspirations of grace. Grace asks very little—only small things, such as keeping silent, rendering a service, overcoming sensitivity, giving a pleasant reply, a smile, and so on. But it never stops asking, and that is what our nature, so subject to change, finds difficult. We soon grow weary of thus renouncing ourselves over and over again.

The best means, the only means of acquiring constancy, of offering ourselves without 'weakening or tiring' is to love Our Lord, with a love that is constantly nourished, renewed and strengthened each morning in our mental prayer, Mass and Holy Communion.

We must store up our supply each morning, 'inflate ourselves' with love for the day, and get ready to give and to sacrifice ourselves. Thus, little by little, our soul is strengthened, our love and our courage grow. We have learnt how to bear up because we have learnt how to love, and to deny ourselves so as to love more deeply."

God was gaining an increasing ascendancy over her. She was being pruned, but not mutilated. He was detaching her progessively, but she was by no means less affectionate: "Sister Marie Thérèse will soon be coming. How I am looking forward to being with her again, with so much in common and so many things to share together."

"At every one of their visits", one of her sisters declared, "Mama and our brothers and sisters found Babeth the same as she always had been. . . . What pleasant, comforting days those were. It was like being really 'together again', with our family affection having grown stronger and more spiritual, and affording us many a happy moment. Even our former gaiety was there . . ."

In community, as soon as Sister Elisabeth learned about another's joys or sorrows, she made them her own. She always found just the right way to express her sympathy, with words that went straight to the heart. By a smile, a kind word, she went out of her way to show the ones with whom she had little contact that they were not forgotten, and that she cared for each one. On feastdays, she would slip in a little word in their own language to the novices who came from other countries.

In a simple manner, easily and quite naturally, she would say a little word about God and turn a conversation to spiritual things. She was somewhat afraid of boring others by speaking about pious things. "Do I speak too much about God at recreation? Yet that's the only thing that can give one real joy."

She was much too good a psychologist not to keep a proper balance, and too supernatural to give the impression of "putting on" and of being exag-geratedly devout. Others did not sense a rich personality imposing its own ideas, or an intellec-tual person giving a dissertation of her favourite topic—although she could have done both. No, she was simply someone who let the excess of her love for God overflow and enrich others.

Her charity, intuitive and attentive, was also expansive and radiantly cheerful. For she had a horror of people with gloomy expressions and affected manners. She liked to stress that humour spoils nothing. She herself had more than her share. She excelled in teasing others—with as much tact as humour. Never was she at a loss for finding, on the spur of the moment, a "scriptural reference" adapted to the most varied incidents and situations.

The other Formation-Aides were well aware to what lengths her imagination could go. The in-firmarian received the latest thing in medical kits, only to find beneath all the wrappings, an assort-ment of . . . old tools. To another, who was to replace Sister Elisabeth in an employment, a legacy in due and proper form announced all the riches she would be inheriting. Not to mention the ad-vance death notices she edited for her companions, the letters bringing sensational news, the telegram announcing the arrival of someone's brother—the addressee never questioning its authenticity . . . and so on.

Who could ever have guessed that, in the depth of her soul, Christ was drawing her to the naked-ness of His Cross? Only by reading between the lines of her letters could this be perceived, here and there, in significant phrases:

"Darkness itself, little everyday sufferings are very necessary. The more we advance, the more we see the reason for the Cross and its place in our lives. Devotedness is praiseworthy, but it is uniquely by suffering that we resemble Our Lord."

She therefore welcomed it under every form, and did so with such cheerfulness that no one could have suspected what immolation the Master was requiring of her day after day, beneath the envelope of what she jokingly called "her carcass" —her poor weary body, already worn out.

A severe deviation of the spinal column was causing her all sorts of discomforts.

If anyone asked about her health, she would smile, as if surprised that anyone should know she was suffering. . . . Except when she would joke about it: "Leaning to the right is my fourth concupiscence. . . . See if I'm not well off!"

To feel sorry for herself never entered her mind.

"It is so sad to see a religious pampering herself and giving in to her feelings. She is like a child who cries when a sacrifice presents itself, who thinks she loves Our Lord, but who doesn't really love Him because she doesn't love His Cross. To become a saint, we must forget ourselves, and we must suffer, paying no attention to what our nature clamours for. When we love Our Lord for Himself alone, we get used to suffering . . ."

She had understood its role, and knew it to be indispensable in the way along which God was leading her. For it was He who had taken the initiative. Paraphrasing a psalm she loved, Psalm 22, she described her own life:

"It is the Lord who is guiding me. . . . The Lord, my God Himself. He is my Shepherd . . . . He is leading me . . . I want for nothing. He has drawn my soul entirely to Himself. In Him, I have everything. The Lord is my Light, my Rest, my Certitude. . . . Though I may walk through a dark valley, even then I will not fear, for He is with me."

Sister Elisabeth had made up her mind to let herself be led on blindly. All the powers of her soul converged toward the idea of offering, that first movement of Christ's humanity—Behold, I Come!

In its light, she penetrated the mystery of the Incarnation, the Eucharistic Sacrifice wherein Christ's attitude of offering is perpetuated, and she wrote:

"To prepare this sacrifice 'to the glory of His holy Name' means, practically speaking, to give oneself entirely, out of love, to God's Will."

To remain thus "entirely offered" was the one and only ambition of her love. There was nothing vague about it. It was a very practical ambition which she clung to, minute by minute. At first, she made certain acts, but gradually rising to a higher level, she aimed only at achieving a permanent attitude, a state of soul. "Keep me as a constant offering to Yourself."

"Jesus, my divine Spouse, my Model, especially in Your offering which was begun, in time, at the moment of the Incarnation, which is perpetuated in the Eucharist, and which is established forever on heaven's altar, I long to unite myself, through Mary, to this ceaseless offering, to become one with it, and let my own become caught up in it."

Jesus, Supreme Offering, help me to aspire unceasingly to this and to achieve it, for it is You who have inspired this longing within me. Suffering, and my years as a religious should have prepared me for it, but my pride is so deep, my selfishness so obstinate. . . . However, with Mary's help, I am confident that it will soon be accomplished.

Jesus, my daily 'leaven', in coming to me, give rise to humility and charity in my heart, to a selfless, total gift of myself. Then I shall be fit for such an offering.

O Jesus, accept me in spite of my weakness and my unworthiness. Take whatever I do not know how to give You. Keep me constantly 'offered' to Yourself, offered to others for Your sake, always through love and for the glory of 'our Father'."

It was an open invitation to the divine invasion . . .

□

God's invasion . . . His Christmas gift to her in 1938.

"Would you believe," she wrote to her brother, "that the reason I'm late in writing to you is because of my Christmas present. On Christmas Eve, the Infant Jesus gave me a 'gift', somewhat overwhelming and absorbing—the direction of the novitiate. You can well imagine that, because this was asked in obedience, my acceptation was prompt and complete, but it was not without some bewilderment which, however, by God's grace, is vanishing little by little. . . . And since then, many pressing obligations have hardly left me a minute.

I beg the help of your prayers so that I may

accomplish the mission God has entrusted to me, among these many novices and postulants. You understand that doing His work requires great detachment, and the sole concern of giving God to souls. I am counting on you."

Two dispositions constituted her program of action, two dispositions that she considered closely related: complete detachment, and the sole concern of giving God to souls. Her Master was coming closer; He was at the door, knocking. Her unexpected nomination was a call to intensify her union with Our Lord and to lose herself in Him.

"We must forget ourselves, deny ourselves, lose ourselves. God is so pleased when we forget about ourselves. The sure and holy way of forgetting self is to put someone else in place of self: Jesus must take over so completely in us that His love absorbs our selfishness.

O Jesus, You want me to be peacefully humble and stripped of self. . . . Only my love for You (which You Yourself will give me) will make me and keep me detached in this way, and completely forgetful of myself.

Like Mary, my Mother, my eminent Model, I should no longer have any personal life of my own. All my life, all my joy is in You, Your Reign, Your Glory, Your Plenitude.

I want to forget my own poverty. I want to enjoy Your Plenitude, and use it to my own advantage. I want to add something to it—you expect me to— by making reparation for consecrated souls especially, by giving myself, and by remaining trustful, entirely abandoned to You no matter what happens, making Your happiness my own."

Dating from this period, her devotion to Mary began to play a greater role in her life. She understood more deeply her interior profile:

"The Blessed Virgin is incomparable. . . . She belongs totally to God.

She is entirely relative to Him. So humble, so like everybody else in her ordinary work in Nazareth. She had little to say, but her love was so pure, her charity so unselfish, and she accepted and endured sacrifices in silence. She knows so well how to help souls become simplified, to go out of themselves, to love without any reservations, without counting the cost . . .

O Mary, so humble, so forgetful and so free of self, teach your child true humility, and that utter forgetfulness of self which is so pleasing in God's sight."

The evening before Babeth's First Holy Communion, her father had copied for her in his fine handwriting the prayer of Father Olier—"O Jesus, living in Mary, come, live in me . . ."

Babeth had treasured it. For a long time she had kept the little piece of paper, torn along the fold and glued back together. She was the only one in the family to have been thus privileged, and the "little ones", with a slight tinge of jealousy, used to look at the enviable treasure but would never dare to ask one for themselves.

As though instinctively, under the sole influence of grace, she came back now to the contemplation of the Sacred Humanity of Jesus in Mary, of the Blessed Virgin's participation in the different stages of her Son's life.

It was in this way that she was to discover the

maternal role of the Mother of Jesus, in all its plenitude.

"O Mary, my Mother, help me to really understand all that the word 'Mother' signifies. Close to you, in you, may I seek the very life of my soul. Be ever more and more a 'Mother' to me, and give me Jesus.

Mother of Grace, form my soul so that I may become a striking, a living image of your firstborn, Jesus, Son of the Eternal Father."

The huge granite edifice of the novitiate at La Tour consists of a central building with four perpendicular wings jutting out. At its furthest end, just at the angle of the fourth wing, was a small room. Its furnishings: a light-chestnut desk, some shelving with a few files, and several chairs with fiber-woven seats.

A small white plaster statue of Our Lady adorned the grey mantlepiece, and on the whitewashed wall facing the desk were two words written in black, "God alone".

A corner of the Breton sky was framed by the window, with its moving, changing colours never quite the same—just like souls. And against this setting, where the beauty of God was stamped from morning until night, tall stately pines towered, stretching up as though reaching for the heavens high above them.

Whenever a light knock sounded at the door, the voice of Mother Elisabeth would answer, "Come in"—with a slight pause between the two words. When the door opened, she would say, "Come". Then silence would fall again—a silence that said better than words that she was waiting for the other one. She was at her disposition, "offered" to her, too selfless to intrude herself between that soul and God or to impose anything personal on her. Free enough, on the contrary, to adapt herself to the other and to accompany her along her path, letting God set the pace, following His lead.

"Father, what I ask, all I desire, is to have within me the same sentiments of Christ Jesus, Your Son and my God. Give me Your Spirit so that I may adhere to all the movements of His Holy Soul."

To be Identified with Him

September 1939. Sister Elisabeth had been Novice Mistress for only nine months, when the upheavals of the war began to be felt in La Tour. International communications had broken down, thus diminishing the number of Sisters for the Second Novitiate, and there was a drop in admissions for the first Novitiate.

The normal routine of the house was completely disorganised. The aged residents evacuated from danger zones and from regions along the coast had moved into the empty quarters of the novices.

Disposing of more time, Sister Elisabeth was put in charge of both Novitiates. Material difficulties

Mother Elisabeth (at right) with her sister,
Sister Marie-Thérèse, in 1939.

abounded, the hospitaller personnel was limited, the novices few. She tried to be as understanding and considerate as she could. Her ability to organize was often sorely tried in an effort to reconcile duty, kindness, and concern for others. At all costs, she wanted to avoid any friction that such a situation could cause. To someone feeling forgotten, she would come proposing something she had already planned.

"I know you have a lot to do today, so I asked Sister X. to replace you for your class."

"After recreation, we are going to continue working in the fields, but would it help you if you were to accompany the few novices who must return before the others?"

When differences of opinion arose, she feared holding too much to her own way of seeing things and would humble herself, deploring her "disgusting selfishness", and her "abominable lack of mortification".

Her days were always fully occupied. The separation of the two novitiates, required by Canon Law, obliged her to go back and forth constantly from one end of the vast building to the other. "I need the gift of bi-location!" she would say jokingly. That was as far as her complaints would go, and she would somehow manage so that nothing was ever left undone.

It was about this time (1942), that she consecrated herself to the Blessed Virgin, using the consecration of Saint Louis-Marie de Montfort. It was the result of a long evolution. As an adolescent, she had preferred to go directly to Jesus without any intermediary, and it was only later that she understood the mediation of Mary. From the moment of this consecration, Our Blessed Lady held a predominant place in her spiritual life, which was becoming more and more clearly defined and orientated: "to have within her the sentiments of Christ Jesus", "to be identified with Him."

"Ever since you have become more truly a part of my life, O Mary, Jesus your Son, and my God, has also become so. Come, be still more a part of my life, and through you, with you, Jesus will invade my poor soul."

On the back of a holy card, she wrote, "Entrust to the most Blessed Virgin Mary your transformation into Jesus. Take refuge in her Heart, in that divine mould which formed Jesus, and will also form you into His likeness."

One year, during the morning of December 8th, one of her assistants received a little note, supposedly written by Our Blessed Lady:

"My child,

I am bringing you a grace, and I am also going to ask you for something—the grace of despoliation, of 'renouncing everything'. I am asking you to put yourself aside, you and all your wretchedness, and to imitate my own selfless life, which didn't belong to itself, so to speak. Jesus Incarnate within me, took complete possession of me, drew me away from myself so that I should live in Him, making His joys my own, His greatness mine, His values my values. May He take you away from yourself so that you can give yourself completely to Him. This is the grace I am bringing you. I will help you to correspond to it.

Mary, Mother of Jesus."

Although not directly occupied with the elderly refugees, Mother Elisabeth was delighted with their presence. She knew each one by name, knew what they were accustomed to, and the tastes of each one. As she went down the corridor of the first floor, which had been converted into an infirmary, there was always someone stopping her at every step, to confide something personal to her. When she would relate their slightest acts and manners, she was inimitable. Her voice, style, facial expressions—nothing was missing in the portraying of a sweet little grandmother's curiosity, trying to pierce the secrets of the novitiate. . . . Escaping supervision, and pretending to be lost, she went into the room where a lesson was being given. Withdrawing most "embarassed", she returned quite satisfied with her exploit and whispered confidentially to her companions, "The novices were keeping quiet. . . . They are being taught silence."

After an alert during the night, she playfully imitated one of the Aged who pleaded between two bursts of gunfire, "Good Mother, quickly—give me some candy before I breathe my last!"

When those listening to her burst out laughing, her goal had been achieved. It was war-time. Everyone, more or less, felt uneasy, and she had to use every means to dispel anxiety. She was so bright and spontaneous that it never occurred to anyone that again, as usual, she had a migraine and that shrugging movement of her shoulders (by then a familiar gesture) betrayed her continual weariness.

She loved both the human and the divine in the Aged, their sublime and their everyday aspects.

She loved them with her whole being—a love that was very human, and yet very supernatural . . . in a word, well-balanced. With a single glance, she could grasp an amusing aspect and also the captivating reality of faith which animates ordinary, everyday events. The first strophe of the Adore Te as applied to hospitality was familiar to her:

"Oh, yes! How very true it is. I adore You, O my God, You who are so truly hidden."

One feast day, in the evening, the novices went to sing for the Aged. During the middle of a song, without saying a word, Mother Elisabeth left them, went across the room to the bedside of one of the sick who was giving some concern. She tried to give her a little drink. Suddenly, she was lost to everything around her and, concentrated on the dying person, she no longer heard anything except the melody of an Adore Te deep within her soul.

For her, hospitaller charity towards the old people was never just a simple, natural compassion for a category of unfortunate and particularly abandoned people, but a real contact with God, a co-operation in His work of Redemption.

"Hospitality is a sure, certain means of forgetting oneself, of leaving oneself behind and of advancing in a truly profound union with Our Lord.

Our Lord has chosen us to participate in His work of Redemption. We should be happy to 'immolate ourselves obscurely and entirely, for the good of souls'. If, in the depths of our souls and of our lives, this thought of faith is there, it will enlighten everything and will keep us from stumbling, from becoming upset in adverse and painful circumstances.

If in prayer it sometimes seems to us that we cannot reach God, we can be certain of reaching Him in our neighbour.

What a degree of union with Our Lord we can attain in our lives of devotedness, if we know how to make this devotedness supernatural, humble, silent, animated by love!

Loving the Poor, loving them as the sacrament which veils Jesus, will enable you to reach Him, to please Him, to show Him that you truly love Him.

Supernatural charity towards the Poor is a wonderful means of forgetting oneself, of acquiring peace of soul and intensifying your love. . . . If there is sacrifice and suffering—and there must be sacrifice and suffering—remember that charity is completed and perfected by sacrifice accepted and offered for souls. . . . It takes a great deal of suffering to convert a soul, Our Lord told little Josefa. We must not refuse to enter fully into the spirit of our vocation, which is the spirit of the Cross.

We love that invitation to be a 'Co-redeemer'. We must love it in reality by living it humbly in the concrete events of our everyday lives . . ."

We find here the same profound desire which was giving more and more unity to her life. Apostolic activity entered into her program of identification. It was towards this conformity that she directed the whole of religious life:

"Realise that by your vocation you must follow Our Lord, becoming another Self for Him.

He is the purpose and the life-principle of our vocation. It was for Him that we came, it is to Him that we have given ourselves, and He alone can satisfy our desires and be our 'infinitely great recompense'.

Why seek elsewhere what He alone can give? Or why be occupied with trifles, self-seeking satisfactions, when by seeking Him, living 'close' to Him, we can already live a deeply happy life on this earth—a life of peace and abandonment in sincere self-forgetfulness for His sake?

You are nothing. Why preoccupy yourself with this 'nothingness'? Forget yourself, efface yourself, don't consider yourself—not even in order to perfect yourself.

Conform yourself to Jesus. Let each day mark a step in this transformation, this identification. That should be the purpose of all your mental prayer, of your Communions, of your desires. May this gradual configuration, sought after, with Our Lord, enlighten and give meaning to all our sacrifices, all our deceptions.

If you really enter deeply and entirely into this work of 'you' becoming 'Jesus', everything will take on meaning, everything will become simpler and easier."

In her letters, she unceasingly came back on this point:

"If, during prayer, we consider our title as religious, if we reflect on what our vocation asks of us . . . we can sometimes feel ashamed of resembling Him so little, of being so preoccupied with ourselves, so sensitive to what touches us.

Be wholly given to Him and, consequently, less and less occupied with yourself. You know what I mean. Take as little account as possible of your 'ego'. Pay no attention to petty, selfish thoughts and sensitive impressions, so as to give Jesus a greater place in your life."

A tiny piece of paper, no bigger than the palm of your hand—most probably the bottom of a half-finished page—brings us a Spiritual Communion which bursts forth like a flame:

"Jesus, for me You took the form of a slave, and You come to me each day in the bareness of a host. Give my soul the grace of this spiritual bareness, of total despoliation, so that soon my soul, stripped of everything for Your sake, may be clothed with You and filled with Your divine Wealth, O You, my God.

O Jesus, Son of the Father, the Word of God, come into my poor soul. Come and accomplish what You will, Your greatest desire: to consume me in 'Unity'.

There where You are, You want me to be with You . . . with the Father, in the unity of Your Spirit.

Tear me away from all that is not Yourself. Detach me from myself so that I may become fit for Your designs of unity and love."

☐

Towards the end of May 1943, the military convoys followed one after the other on the roads hardly ever used bordering the novitiate garden. Bombings had destroyed the railways, buses had stopped running. It was impossible to reach La Tour. At the last minute, the priest who was expected to give the retreat before profession could not come.

Obliged to prepare the novices herself, Mother Elisabeth jotted down in a note-book an outline for twenty-four conferences. Notes that were necessarily impersonal, but everything in them centered on the subject of identification. She was following the natural bent of her own soul.

The form remained didactic, although here and there a phrase, a quotation, an ejaculation escaped, letting her own soul shine through:

"Jesus, my Model of sanctity, Model given me by the Father. . . . For Your sake I should be famished for holiness. May I become identified with His life as the Son. May I become identified with that incessant 'movement of Love' which, in the Holy Spirit, carries Him to the Father.

The state of grace is identification with Someone.

Holiness is a life, a mystery of divine life given and received, sustained, nourished. . . . My many miseries need this divine contact, to cling to Him, to drink in His humility, His charity. I can enter thereby into participation with what the Father has given Jesus, and what is the greatest of all things—His Sonship.

Into Your Hands, O Lord, more than ever, I commend my soul, my life. 'Your Hands' . . . Hands that are creative and infinitely mighty, that have formed me, that have modelled my life until now and will continue to form me—if I am faithful and confident—into the likeness of Your Well-beloved Son.

This confidence, this abandonment, this immobility in Your hands, is the expression of a love that wants to be entirely for You: pure, free, divested of all self-seeking."

□

One day, following a series of slides on the Holy Face and the Shroud of Turin, the conversation came back on this subject. Some of the Sisters regretted that there was a certain lack of historical facts which would have enabled them to appreciate this mysterious object at its true value. Mother Elisabeth reacted. With astonishing conviction and enthusiasm she retorted, "But there's no doubt about it. . . . It's certain!"

Although she did not much like holy pictures, she made an exception for reproductions of the Holy Face. "Every religious should have a picture of the Holy Face . . . it is the only true portrait of Our Lord."

It was before this Face "disfigured" by her sins that she wrote:

"Face of Jesus, Face veiled as though disfigured by my sin, hide me in the 'secret of Your Face'. May I there at last learn this difficult lesson: to love to be hidden, unknown, forgotten, and counted as nothing . . .

Sorrowful, humiliated Face . . . make me understand realistically that to truly love means to forget oneself and to die to self.

Hidden Jesus, having become the 'least of men' . . . teach me how to be sincerely humble and detached from myself, and live fully within me."

"May Jesus, 'Radiance of the Father's Splendour and Image of His Substance,' Jesus who, in view of the joy that was reserved for Him chose the ignominy of the cross, may He make you love your limitations and your helplessness, and even your weaknesses. May He give us to understand and to experience that it is in this total divesting and this loss of self-independence that a soul is enriched with God, and experiences an abundance of peace."

She often insisted on the necessity of "asking for a sense of sin". She quoted a passage from a book by Father A. Hanrion: "My God, give me the courage and the peace necessary to allow You not only to destroy sin but also its accomplices. . . . When I feel a new destruction, O joyous peace— it is an accomplice of sin, an enemy of the Holy of Holies that is disappearing. O Jesus, Victorious God, Living God, I adore You."

The verse of the Miserere: "Do not turn your face from me", was particularly dear to her, as was also the text from Isaiah: "We were all unclean, and all our justice was like soiled clothing. . . ."

This way of seeing things was habitual to her: "Often I say to myself how I make the yoke of the Lord heavy and burdensome." The affirmation was sincere. However, those close to her deny the fact.

"She overflowed with the love of God.[1] The intensity of His life within her drew others along. Sometimes she would express it by exclaiming 'How I long to see Him. I am weary of what is created.' Yet for the same creatures, she made herself all to all. One day when the Blessed Sacrament was exposed, she told me, 'I wanted so badly to go to the chapel, but I thought to myself that the novices would be glad to see me, so I made the sacrifice. . . . We must never seek ourselves in anything. When we do, we find ourselves, but when we put ourselves aside to please others, we find

God. There are souls who will never find Him in the chapel, because they do not know how or do not want to find Him there where He is hidden—in our neighbour, in our duty.'

Whenever I met her in the corridors, she would look at me in case I needed to speak to her. That was pure charity, for I knew how much, inwardly, she dreaded being made late. One day she involuntarily revealed it by remarking: 'I am going to the infirmary. I'm almost afraid of meeting someone on the way who may make me late.'

One of her maxims was that 'vigour' must characterize the soul of a religious who is detached. (Often she repeated a passage from the Book of Judith, 'Thou hast done manfully, and thy heart has been strengthened.') She reproached me for my tears when she discerned self-pity. 'You know, you weaken yourself when you let yourself go like that, pitying yourself.' Her great virility did not prevent her from being immensely understanding, compassionate towards moral depression caused by physical or nervous fatigue. She told me that she had once wept from lassitude at the beginning of a period of convalescence, the first day that the infirmarian had helped her out of bed and into a chair for a few hours: 'I learned a lot then. Physical fatigue excuses many things. One reaches the point where nothing can be supported without crying. Certain souls need encouragement.' And one evening before a feast day she invited me, 'Come to my room tomorrow. I shall read you a thought from Saint John of the Cross.' (Her choice was in-

---

[1] Testimony of one of her assistants.

evitably something about detachment). 'Have you seen my Infant Jesus? (a holy card in her missal). I will show it to you. He seems to be saying, 'Keep up your courage, my child.' She passed it to me the next morning, right in the chapel, I think.

To help with formation, she gave great latitude, avoiding whatever would seem to be an appearance of superiority. 'The Good Lord does good by whomsoever He wants. . . . We are so insignificant.'

When I began to give the classes, she went through them with me, corrected, made suggestions, then left me with the impression that I had done wonders. After the class, she would be looking for me to ask, 'Did it go all right this morning?' If she noticed some preoccupation in my expression, she used to ask, (You're not worrying too much, are you? I hope it's not I who am bothering you?'

One particular semestre, there were only three novices for the next profession. I was in admiration seeing her put so much heart into 'preaching to her trio', as she would say. She answered, 'If there were only one to understand and to whom to show the way, I would not have wasted my time . . . three souls are worth as much as a hundred.'

It would be impossible to forget the conviction in her voice while she was explaining the Constitutions: 'It is unthinkable that a Little Sister would not have great zeal for souls. You haven't come here for yourselves, to ponder over your miseries, but rather for Our Lord, for souls. We are afraid of sacrifice. Now you must make your choice: all or nothing. And if you are not ready to sacrifice yourself, it would be better not to continue.' "

Mother Elisabeth preached by her example.

Always dissatisfied with her interior life, she sought God through renunciation:

"In renouncing something, we come closer to Him, and that is all that matters!

Nothing equals the gift of true renunciation, inspired by love. By it, we unite ourselves to Our Lord without any risk of illusion.

The greater our legitimate ambition to find Our Lord, to give Him, to make reparation for others and to glorify Him, the more we must be prepared to walk the path of faith, abandonment and true renunciation."

She kept watch over herself, asking one of her close collaborators to indicate what needed rectifying in her. "We must follow ourselves closely", she said, "so as to give our religious life all it deserves."

With virile frankness she would render the same service to others, through love of "the truth": "How we should love the truth, 'act in truth', never be afraid of it—it is the one thing which gives flavour to everything. I approve of showing appreciation to souls, so that they feel we have confidence in them." She herself encouraged: "You are a great help to me. You should never be sad, you are a soul who is seeking Our Lord." She corrected also: "You let your feelings get the better of you. You get indignant about certain limitations; take care—it's noticeable."

With acute awareness, in "the truth", she perceived the majesty and the sanctity of God:

"We are serving a Great Master."

"Make sure you realize that you have not given yourself to 'just anybody'."

In a notebook, after the passage from the Book of Revelation, "They rest not day or night, crying, Holy, holy, holy", she added, "Let me know who You are, my God, so that I may better understand what You want." Several quotations from the Old Testament on the sanctity of God followed, then she finished with a prayer:

"My God, You are Love and Your sanctity is this faithfulness of the sovereign and immutable love with which You love the Sovereign Good that You Yourself are, O my God. It is by loving that my love will become purer, freer, O my God, and the more I share in Your sanctity, the more I shall keep myself holier for You, my God."

☐

This "identification", the very reason of her existence—Mother Elisabeth sensed that it must be accomplished "in solitude".

When the time came for the annual retreat, she sighed, "I hope the conferences won't be too long. I would love to have a retreat in solitude."

Three pages of a blue notebook—that of her retreat in 1943—are dedicated to this theme:

"I will lead her into the desert and I will speak to her heart." (Hosea)

"It is God Himself who leads a soul into solitude —no one but He can do it—He and the soul alone. My soul should, under the influence of grace, do its part.

My God, teach me to descend into the depth, into the centre of my soul, into this 'Holy of Holies' where things human, sensitive impressions, the noise of earth cannot reach.

Help me to pass beyond that 'threshold' where things created generate noise and agitation, and to come to the place where You dwell. Teach me how to descend there, to remain there 'alert in my faith', in my love, attentive to listen to You and faithfully respond to You, saying 'yes', 'ecce', to all that You ask, to all the demands of Your Love."

> *"VACATE . . . Learn to remain empty, alone, detached. . . . ET VIDETE: you will see, you will experience that I alone am Infinite . . . your God . . . He who surpasses all your expectation and who has no equal."*

Towards Him Who Surpasses All Our Expectations

The sky was heavy with snow on the octave-day of the Epiphany, 1945. The rationing of coal prevented the central heating from functioning. Despite the makeshift heaters, the old people, still at La Tour, shivered with cold in the vast rooms of the novitiate.

Mother Elisabeth's hands were chapped and swollen with chillblains. Her room, where there was no fire, was glacial. After having received the novices for the greater part of the day, she replied to one of her correspondents:

LA TOUR SAINT-JOSEPH
January 13th, 1945

". . . You must, absolutely, hold firm in your prayer life. It is in prayer that you will find strength, that you will form a supernatural and religious attitude and, little by little, that you will find Our Lord and love Him.

It is He, and He alone, whom you need, for whom you hunger. . . . Do not look behind, and do not waver from your purpose. On the contrary, it is by holding fast to it that you will be at peace and that you will learn to taste the sweetness of Christ's yoke.

It will take you some time to overcome the difficulties of your temperament and your former habits, but what does that matter, when you know also that the sacrifices and sufferings you will meet are beneficial both for yourself and for souls . . .

Seek Our Lord untiringly and you will find Him —and all else together with Him. . . . Remain obstinately trusting and joyful . . .

What distinguishes a fervent religious from a mediocre religious is the steady and firm will, always determined to put duty first, to accept sacrifice and, if necessary, to bear up under weariness, under the Cross."

To seek, strive, wait for, hold on to . . . absolutely, untiringly, obstinately. . . . Mother Elisabeth said it, wrote it, repeated it—and repeated it to herself especially, over and above everything:

"A saint, you know, is an obstinate being."

"What is lacking in many souls is that they do not know how to wait."

To know how to wait for God . . . even if it meant waiting in the darkness of night, like the nights which fell so quickly those January evenings. But to wait however, with great yearning:

"In the presence of this great God of yours, be as one famished, hungering for Him, enduring this hunger and desire for Him alone. . . . May He be the unique object of the incessant searching of your soul. This ardent desire, overshadowing all else, concentrated on Him, is in itself pure praise . . ."

To wait prayerfully:

"To pray is to assure the continuity of one's effort; it is to remain determined to be victorious; it is, finally, to arrive progressively at a true, intimate union with Our Lord.

The Holy Spirit is calling you to dwell in the depths of your soul, and to unite yourself, in the silence of adoration and of love, to the Three Divine Persons who make your soul their Temple, the Holy Place, the witness of their mutual exchanges."

Above all, to wait alone, in silence:

"The further the soul progresses, the more simple it becomes, and the less it has to say, because it is coming closer to God and because silence alone unites it with Him.

Facing God alone, His Design, His Will, the soul goes to Him in silence and solitude . . .

In God, in Him alone, be silent, my soul. With others, poor human words are necessary, 'which begin and end all'. With your great God, no— 'His true praise is silence'. He is beyond and defies all praise. . . . Let all within you become deep silence, bowed down in adoration and love. Remain without wanting anything, without any desire, seeking nothing but Him. Let all your being be still before Him Alone."

"My help and my Model is the Blessed Virgin of the Incarnation. Go to her, imitate her 'Nescivi', her waiting, her desires."

During the time of the visit to the Blessed Sacrament, the gallery of the chapel was usually empty. That made it the preferred place of Mother Elisabeth.

"When I am there, I enter into silence . . . I no longer hear anything."

Often she was to be seen kneeling on the floor, making the Way of the Cross. That was, for her, communion with the suffering Heart of Christ, a powerful means of penetrating the mysteries of His Sacred Soul, of forgetting herself, of leaving herself so as to love Him, to console Him, to share His solitude.

"It is in seeing Our Lord reduced to nothing," she wrote, "that one becomes peaceful in suffering, learns total detachment . . . in this stripping, in this loss of all self-sufficiency, the soul becomes enriched by God . . ."

When Mother Elisabeth descended the narrow stone staircase from the gallery, she still had an absorbed expression. It was obvious that she had to make a real effort to return to exterior realities.

□

At the end of 1945, the novitiate took on again its former aspect. Mother Elisabeth no longer had the responsibility of the Second Novitiate on her shoulders. But at this beginning of the post-war period, a lack of recruits was deeply felt, and was painfully hard for her to bear.

Was she not partly responsible? Was she not placing obstacles in the work of "her Master"?

Were not the shortcomings of the novices due to her own deficiencies? She was convinced that such was the case: "I believe that if there was a saint in my place, things would go better."

After reprimands where she had shown a resolute firmness, the feeling of her own insufficiency made her add, "Pray for me, that I will be equal to my duty."

For seven years now, she had been carrying out this duty.

Physically she had suffered, and had aged a great deal, though continuing to make little of her constant maladies: "We shall always have something to suffer. We must forget ourselves and act as though nothing were the matter."

Intellectually, she had gained much experience. Spiritually, she had fixed her ideal of identification and the path of detachment which led there.

In her attitude towards others, it seemed that she was continually watchful to efface herself in order to create a direct contact between God and them. "We must be impersonal, never wanting to lead souls by our own ways. The Little Sisters must never be able to guess our own personal spiritual inclinations. It is very difficult not to say anything which alludes to the 'me', but in my opinion, we must at least strive towards this." Not that this prevented her in any-way from giving clear, firm and precise counselling.

Her rare quality of understanding, already the result of psychological tact and judgment refined by seven years of experience, can only really be explained by her extreme self-renunciation. It enabled her natural intellectual and affective qualities to be used to the utmost degree in order to adjust to the capacity of souls and, ultimately, to adjust herself to God's designs.

That was her aim: to identify herself with God's plan for souls, so as to help them to discover and achieve what He expected of them. She could do that only by completely disregarding her own views, anything that might turn to her own advantage, however legitimate. Her constant concern was to convey the truth to souls.

If she had formed the conviction that a purely contemplative form of life was feasible for one of her novices who, though perfectly expansive and happy, had confided to her an attraction to a cloistered life sacrificed in view of a more total gift, Mother Elisabeth straightaway helped her to discern her possibilities.

She would have reproached herself had she not, in all loyalty, helped this soul discover the life of union that Our Lord was asking of her, and the facilities she could have found to achieve it, in a contemplative order.

"What I particularly admired in her," said one of her former novices, "was the liberty she left us with God. She respected His designs even in the smallest details."

For her, the great proof of love is fidelity. She knew her novices were being called to live a laborious life. She wanted them to be very devoted, practical, given to duty. "Beautiful thoughts are nothing," she said to her assistants. They must understand to what degree renunciation should be at the base of our lives." She exacted of her novices vigour and fidelity.

Her will to be identified with God's designs however, tempered the very absolute tendency of her own character, that severity concerning the novices about which she reproached herself nevertheless, to the very end. There was no longer the eagerness, rather too natural, to see souls rapidly being transformed.

The more she "became identified", the more everything within her became harmonious, balanced and serene. She appeared, at one and the same time, very vigorous and very sensitive; energetic, without weakness and possessed of unwearing kindness; simple, and profoundly religious in her ways; taken up with God, yet full of practical good sense; supernatural in everything, yet remaining most human.

It would seem that her radiance—we could even say her ascendancy—was due above all to her simple, attractive and thoughtful charity. Its source was in her union with Our Lord, and she would forget about herself with such apparent ease and lack of effort that it seemed quite natural.

In her desire to be in conformity with God's design for each soul, she acquired the gift of knowing how to listen, to penetrate the thoughts of others, untiringly, with an interest which was neither feigned nor conventional, but sincere and most real.

Without any hint of condescension, she put herself on the same level as others, seeming to be very close to them because she still knew how to see and think with the eyes and soul of a postulant or a novice. To put them at ease, to break the ice, she would tease or make a comical reflection, even during silence time.

She was full of life, ardent, her blue eyes at times grave, at other times enthusiastic, sometimes mischievous, and "her smile always lit up her expression and gave others the impression of sharing a joy, delightful to feel." [1]

"She was so sensitive that it seemed as though she felt what we were feeling, but with extreme discretion. Very foresighted and intuitive, with sure judgment, she could grasp what we were going through, showing us just a hint of it, and that helped us to be expansive, seeing how she could guess things. Even by the tone of her voice in pronouncing your name, you could tell that you were loved and esteemed." [2]

Her affection for her novices was not "disembodied". So mortified herself, she was full of thoughtfulness and consideration for others, especially to help them bear their difficulties and sacrifices. To a remark made about her special charity towards the sick, she replied, "You know, when one of them is suffering, I step out of my role of correcting. My only desire is to bring relief. . . . For me, there is no longer a novice, but someone who is suffering."

It was not by analogy with an external and affective comportment that she was maternal, but rather, first of all, in the reality of the gift of her vital powers for the transmission of life.

When her novices were questioned, one of them replied: "In seeing her, one thought of the Great-

---

[1] Testimony of a novice.

[2] Testimony of a novice.

ness of the God who had invaded her. At prayer, during the Office, it was striking to see the depth of her recollection. The very tone of her voice led us to God . . . and her bearing, always so mortified and firm. You could sense that she was established in a serenity of soul which nothing could alter. One day she said, 'Even if everything around us should crumble, what could trouble us? The Good Lord is within us.' "

Another described "her way of judging everything in the light of eternity", and told of a reflection she overheard one November 2nd: "When I see the catafalque, I ask God to let me see all things now as I will see them when I shall be beneath it."

And again: "A soul which sounded the depths of everything, especially of humility, of the love of suffering. . . . You could feel that suffering had chiselled her—she spoke to us about the Cross with expressions which almost made us afraid: "The cross which does not make us fall to the ground is no cross at all. Our Lord wanted, as it were, to be unable to measure up to the task during the Passion—even though He was God, He willed to be crushed by His Cross."

"What was immediately striking in Mother Elisabeth was the perfect harmony of her authority and her humility. In receiving an avowal from someone, she always answered in the first person, as though she was the one in question: 'We're not worth much, are we! You and I, we're both alike."

One last note, very true: "In all her actions there was a 'finished touch', a concern for 'perfection'. Neither fastidiousness nor scrupulosity, but a desire to do all things well, like her "Great Master.' "

Mention was also made of her "high esteem for our vocation . . . we owe her a lot, but above all to have had inculcated within us the spirit of the Congregation—complete littleness, and the absolute gift of self."

To form her novices to be authentic daughters of Jeanne Jugan, she herself showed them how to live her spirit, by her own example. She kept in her desk a copy of the Acts of the Diocesan Process of Information, and sometimes she would quote from it—preferably a quote touching on humility, renunciation or abnegation. "For years, Sister Marie de la Croix underwent a real moral torture, without ever letting anyone see in her either a gesture or a word of impatience or discontent. On the contrary, she tried to hide her interior suffering from others. God was the only one to know of them."

Those who knew Mother Elisabeth could testify that she herself lived our Mother's counsels in her own life.

During this period when there were only a few novices, she used her free time to improve her knowledge of Holy Scripture. She drew deeply from it, with a joy that was always new. In this domain, everything was nourishment for her receptive soul. She was so anxious to "know" God! Her conferences were enriched in solidity and in substance.

Of all these preferred texts, she assimilated above all the Letter to the Hebrews. She had a thorough knowledge of it and wanted to help others appreciate it. Because it is a sacerdotal epistle, it corresponded to her interior attraction to pray for priests. For the same reason, she loved the prayers

of the Mass of Our Lord Jesus Christ, Eternal
High Priest.

Her love for the prayer of the Church, together
with her love for all that was beautiful, attracted
her to the liturgy. To explain the devotion to the
Sacred Heart and the spirit of reparation (which
she called, "the magnificent, but austere duty of
true reparation"), she used only the texts of the
Mass Cogitationes.

Her enthusiasm for certain verses of the psalms
became communicative: "Dominus regnavit, deco-
rem indutus est . . . Vacate et videte . . . Nonne
Deo subjecta . . ." and in a very personal manner,
she translated: "In God alone my soul is stilled."
This was not surprising. Irresistibly, her dominant
attraction led her to texts concerning silence and
solitude. She pointed out the beauty of the little
known Mass text of Our Lady of the Cenacle, all
about solitude of heart. A book on the writings of
Saint Albert the Great was passed on with a recom-
mendation: ". . . above all, the chapter on solitude
of heart" . . . the page was marked.

Most significant is this prayer she composed and
sent for a feastday:

"O Jesus, Son of the Father, of 'our Father',
hear the ardent prayer of my soul. Grant that I may
perfectly die to myself so that You alone may live
in me. Grant that I may keep an interior silence as
profound as that of the dead, so that You alone
may speak to my heart.

May I remain in stillness, so that You can bring
about in me all that You desire . . .

O Jesus, possess all the powers of my soul, keeping them so securely within Yourself, O Word of

God, that I may become 'one spirit with You' . . .

May the Father, 'our Father', finding 'His Christ' in my soul, be filled with delight and receive therein, 'through Him, with Him and in Him, all honour and glory'."

To render to the Father 'all honour and glory' and in order that 'His praise be complete', she must participate in all the states of her Christ. Mother Elisabeth's soul went forward, step by step, ever a pilgrim, always advancing, "the best of herself straining towards the End to which she aspires", ambitious to "adhere to all the movements" of the Soul of Christ, to become "one same spirit with Him".

What stage had she reached in her "conformity" with Him? Had she even begun? And this idea haunted her: "to begin" at last.

We see her, sitting at her desk one feast day, when the rigor of habitual silence is interrupted. Someone knocked. To receive the one who was entering she straightened herself, turned towards the door, and the Little Sister bringing the morning's mail entered her room.

Mother Elisabeth was in a half-light, her frail silhouette against the white wall, a light in her eyes and in her smile. Slowly, she slipped her hands into the large sleeves of her habit, and in a half-serious, half-playful tone of voice, stressing each word, said without further preamble, "Well then, Sister, when are we really going to 'begin'?"

We find still, as always, the theme of identification recurring in letters written around this time:

". . . Everything has meaning in a life consecrated to Our Lord, in a life which, day by day, leads us towards holiness and transformation into Him. . . . You have so many means of sustaining this 'obstinate hunger' for perfection, if you want it really, above all else . . .

This desire for holiness is itself a grace that we must ask from Our Lord. It comes from Him, and every Communion gives us the principle of holiness, the One 'who Alone is Holy'.

Unite yourself intimately to the Holy Soul of Jesus who is within you by the Host, and little by little, through the action of the Host you receive daily, you will become 'holy', you will achieve integrally His plan for you. Our life is given to us only for that. . . . Blessed is the soul who enters this way and who understands that the sole thing for her, the secret of her strength and her happiness, the meaning of her life, is this progressive transformation into Jesus, identification with Him . . .

Keep Our Lord always before your eyes. Ask Him, above all, to fill your soul and give you this insatiable need of Him which transforms life, snatches the soul from her selfishness and surrenders it without reserve to thanksgiving. To avoid the illusion of selfishness, which can hide itself even in this desire for Our Lord, be attentive that each of your acts of love be accompanied by renunciation."

Identification . . . Solitude . . . this is truly "her grace". She follows this direction ever more and more. Everything which could attract her, hold her back for an instant (she was so well-loved) seemed, on the contrary, to increase her detachment and her separation. "Life is made up of sacrifice and detachment and, little by little, the Good Lord teaches us to seek nothing but Him alone. . . . May your whole being, before Him, enter this great silence which is His Dwelling; may all your powers be stilled, and may all other desire, regret, choice, fear and everything similar disappear and be extinguished before this great Divine Majesty who wants to invade everything, to subdue everything, who wants you wholly His. . . . Sing to Him this beautiful praise of a soul pacified, detached, silent. May the Holy Spirit Himself create within you this pure praise . . ."

Nonetheless, she loved her work; oh, how she loved it! In September 1947, she wrote to one of her assistants, recently named Mother Mistress of Novices:

"We are then going to remain in communion by our charge and our prayers. . . . Mine will sollicit for you . . . intimate, profound union with Our Lord, encountered in detachment, and in complete surrender of ourselves. Isn't this the only thing to desire, which alone makes life and all its suffering worthwhile? All the rest is deceptive, except Him or what is done for His sake . . ."

A month later, to the same Sister:

". . . How happy I am to know that you are doing so well and wholly given to your duty, there where God wants you to be. There you are going to find many joys, difficulties and deceptions also, for any responsibility carries these, isn't it true? However, your task of formation particularly brings true joys and true sufferings: the joy of seeing souls open to Our Lord, to make Him loved by them, to help them enter into full understanding of their vocation . . . suffering also, not to be able to render souls capable of giving everything one would want them to for His glory, and to be oneself so little like one should be.

As you said so well, the Blessed Virgin, our Mother and Mistress, presides and acts in our name. What a source of peace and true happiness! How well you do to give her so large a place in the novitiate, the first after Jesus, proceeding from Him: His Mother."

The following spring, Mother Elisabeth wrote again, always to the same Sister:

". . . I am happy for you that the novitiate is getting on so well, that it is prospering. I would even be a little jealous of the growing number of novices, if I weren't so interested in you, but how could I be jealous of my former companion for whom I have wished the best of graces and fullest success in the task confided to her! Everything is fine then, isn't it?

That this visit [1] has renewed for you the suffering of being so far away, does not surprise me. But on the other hand, in growing older, the soul sometimes likes to be a little alone, deprived (only partly) of human support, and to have to confide herself to, and find rest in God alone. The God we love is truly the Almighty, and He lends His strength to the soul who counts on Him. . . . I am sure you are experiencing this more and more.

Don't be worried about me . . . [2] I'll hold on, and get over this spell, you'll see. There is still a

[1] Short visit of Mother General.
[2] She had just been ill.

great need to remain on this earth and leave here our selfish linings. Our Lord knows that well. It is good to be fashioned by Him, to discover each day more of our own ugliness and of His greatness, and to teach ourselves how to love Him!

It is wonderful too, isn't it, to teach others how to love Him? I'm sure you feel that joy deeply. It is accompanied by suffering, to be sure, because we don't see every soul opening to the light in the same degree and responding fully to grace. I wish you many consolations in this domain.

Right now, we are reading the life of Charles de Foucauld in the refectory, and his writings in the oratory. His writings are really thoughts directed to God, very beautiful and very simple — true prayers. And so simple that they're almost child-like, and that does us good.

The Dominicans have published an issue of the "Vie Spirituelle" which is a penetrating study of the doctrine of Dom Marmion, of his 'Christo-centrism'. All in all, it is an analysis of his life and his doctrine, which can be summed up in these words, 'Jesus is everything for me'. What a master Dom Marmion is, and how beautiful his works, so full of Our Lord!"

Every year, the month of December was the time for the annual retreat. Those during these years, and of 1946 especially, were a torment for Mother Elisabeth. But her principle remained the same as for her spells of illness: cut short immediately any turning in on self. On this subject, no personal notes.

She practised what she wrote:

"Unworthy, you certainly are. . . . Bury yourself

in your nothingness. Count only on His grace, His mercy, on the all powerful Word which in an instant can and wants to transform your soul, if only—despising yourself and surrendering yourself entirely—you know how to give yourself up to His divine action . . .

It is Jesus who brings and gives you everything: 'His Body, His Soul, His Divinity, His Mysteries, His Sufferings and His Glories.'

Through Him, you have access to the Father. In Him, you are raised up and loved by the Father."

Some enlightening phrases were found, dating from Christmas 1947, and they can easily be recognised as her own: it is a little letter supposedly written by the Infant Jesus:

"To be My Joy, to be the Joy of your God: what a great ambition—to which your vocation, 'My choice' itself invites you!

My grace this Christmas will help you to achieve it. Look at Me: if God could take this Delight, His Joy in my Holy Humanity, it was because this Humanity, without its own personality, adhered totally to the Word, without reserve, without regret and, carried away thus to the Bosom of the Father, lived by Him, without its own activity, without personal self-seeking, without anything of itself.

So it is that you must become nothing, remain nothing, if you want to enter into My Joy, and to be My Joy.

Jesus."

And again, undated, this prayer:
"O Word of God, reveal to me the meaning of

this phrase, and its mysterious attraction: 'the Bosom of the Father'.

Your dwelling, 'our' dwelling, since it is Your will to share it with us. It was You Yourself who said, 'I will that where I am, they also should be.'

May my soul be silent, may Your Divine Spirit, 'Consuming Fire', purify it, detach it, transform it, 'accustom it' to his Divine Milieu. May my soul, by uniting itself to You through faith and love, participate in that Eternal Gaze which You fix on Your Father.

Grant also that my soul may merit, by the grace of adoption, to be looked upon, seen 'in You' by the Father and become caught up in the incessant movement of Love of Your Divine Spirit.

O Mary, my Mother, be my 'Forma Dei'. Keep me well hidden in this other Dwelling of the Incarnate Word, your blessed womb, so that my soul will there receive the 'stamp' of Jesus, the Beloved Son, for the Glory of the Father through the action of the Spirit of Love."

This mysterious attraction for the "Bosom of the Father" gave her soul a real nostalgia for her "Divine Milieu" to the point where she admitted: "When I am all alone, I feel like crying out my desire to go there."

□

*"The Spirit will be your serene
and tranquil strength, and through
Him you will support the action of
Infinite Love who has chosen your
poor little soul for His Praise and
Glory."*

For His Praise and Glory

Mother Elisabeth wrote these lines for Pentecost,
1948. As her correspondence during April gives
us to understand, she had just gone through "a
difficult stretch" and she was only half-way towards
recovery.

After several days of rest, she had, nevertheless,
resumed her daily conferences and, as each year,
she spent half the night between Holy Thursday
and Good Friday near the Altar of Repose. She
loved this night of prayer in the same way as she
loved the Holy Hour on the eve of every First
Friday. These were hours of silence and solitude,
and to fill them with an unending stream of vocal

prayers seemed to her to be a mistake: "No," she said, "that is not what Our Lord asked for."

To continue leading a life like everyone else, she had to summon up all her energy—but without illusions all the same. "Infinite Love" had chosen her soul for "his Praise and Glory". She knew it, and wanted only to see His plan carried out:

"May He be glorified . . . I have asked Him to identify me with Himself, no matter what the cost, no matter how . . .

Is this independence, or presumption? No, I don't think so. He knows very well that I can do nothing without Him, and that I always count on His grace. Besides, I want nothing outside of obedience."

This obedience was her strength. Her love for everything she knew to be "the intentions" of her Superiors, sustained her more than anything else. She could hardly take any nourishment; she was becoming weaker, and every effort weighed on her.

To be obliged to spare herself, to no longer be able to follow the common pace, to have exemptions and dispenses—God knows what it cost her!

Joyous "usque ad mortem", she laughed at her wretchedness. "You'll see, I'll die laughing." Another day, somewhat teasingly, she said, "You will let me die alone and without the Sacraments." To be sure, everyone protested, and no one took her seriously.

Her state of physical depression made her more sensitive, more apt to experience interior suffering.

Towards, the middle of June, she wrote,

"The Father makes you powerfully strong by His Spirit . . . in view of the interior nature . . .

This new effusion of the 'Spirit of Love' is a gift of the Father . . . in view of the interior nature . . . for a new step forward . . .

'His love is strong as death.' He destroys so as to infuse a richer life. He abases and annihilates so as to enable growth, and to fill the soul beyond measure.

The Spirit will be your serene and tranquil strength, and through Him you will support the action of Infinite Love who has chosen your poor little soul for His Praise and Glory."

Mother Elisabeth is aware that, for her also, the Spirit will be her "serene and tranquil strength" for a new step forward.

At recreation on the first Sunday of July, she wanted to read the letter that Saint Ignatius wrote while a prisoner, to the Christians of Rome. Those around her were against it, because reading aloud tired her. She teased, "Look at that! I can no longer do my own will!" And, for once, she did not give in. When reading the last lines, "I no longer have in me anything to be burnt away, there is left only living water which cries out, 'Come to the Father,'" did she realise she had given expression to her own soul?

Although she was well cared for and surrounded with every attention, her health was declining. July brought no improvement, nor did August. When, at the end of the month, Mother Elisabeth had to give up activity altogether, the latest attacks, violent ones, having left her exhausted, she had greatly altered.

She did everything she could to try to appear better than she was: hiding with a smile the effort she made to rise from her armchair whenever she saw a Superior, and welcoming all the more cordially if she sensed that the one wishing to enter her room was hesitant or feared to intrude. "Come now, I'm so happy to see you . . . you did well to come."

Her illness gave her the occasion of perfecting the practice of obedience. At times she reproached herself for having gone "a little too far", believing sincerely that she "could support more". "For the past ten years," she avowed, "I have been putting on a comedy." Her consolation was to have been quite open about her spells of ill-health of the last few years: "I am happy to have spoken up. It is by God's permission that I am suffering so much and that nothing could be found to give me relief."

Since there seemed to be no improvement in sight, there was question of the Sacrament of the Sick. She was informed, and calmly asked,

"Do you think I am going to die?"

"I don't think you will, straightaway."

"Neither do I . . . I ask your pardon if I have hurt you in any way . . . it was quite involuntary."

Then, after a moment's silence, as though speaking to herself, she said, "I truly believe that I have never sought anything other than to lead souls to Him."

□

At the beginning of October, it seemed preferable to transfer her to the infirmary. She sensed that this separation from the novitiate was definitive. Who would have thought so? She was heart-broken, and she sobbed. An instant later, her serenity regained, she humiliated herself because of "this real weakness".

Her great worry was not being able to receive easily those who wanted to see her. It tormented her. In spite of violent headaches which nothing could calm and which prevented her even from praying, she was most anxious about giving all facilities to the Formation Aides to use her books and her notes: "Don't hesitate, take anything you want . . . nothing is mine."

According to a comparison she had often used, she tried "to be beneath the wine-press as though not being there." When a Little Sister returned from the hospital, Mother Elisabeth straightaway sent her a word of welcome, the promise of her prayers and of a neighbourly visit as soon as possible. As soon as she felt somewhat better, off she went, as cheerful as she was unsteady on her feet.

"I am praying for you . . . you'll get better . . ."

"So will you, Mother."

"Me? I'm too old!"

And she left, laughing. During the course of conversation, she had promised the sick Little Sister a picture of the Holy Face. When she had permission to offer it, she returned and, with her usual thoughtfulness, let her choose among four reproductions.

To give pleasure to a Polish novice, she asked to have read at recreation an article on the Cardinal Primate of Poland. From her bed, she sent her feastday wishes to this one and that one, and sent short notes, little instructions:

October 1st. "Good evening! Have you spent a good day of reparation? I hope so, and I hope too that the apple picking gave you some good occasions to give of yourself and to offer up.

Tomorrow, you could spend this day of preparation with our Blessed Mother, and live with her and in her an intense day of interior prayer, recollected in those depths where the Good Lord dwells, where He reveals Himself, where He asks and calls us also . . .

Make the firm resolution to offer through Mary, to the Sacred Heart, three acts of real humility. That is what He loves and expects from us. You know that already, and it is the best means to glorify Him and to 'force' Him to grant you abundant graces.

My thought for you, from Saint Paul: 'Seek holiness, without which no one will see the Lord.'

Holiness, that is to say, union with God through grace and love, is the condition imposed by Himself in order to see Him in the next life in Glory, to see Him already here on earth by a more enlightened faith, by a richer and more intense grace.

Let each one of us set to work to pursue, to seek this holiness."

Persuaded that she had done nothing for the novitiate, she believed herself to be truly poor and without any merit: "The Good Lord has no need of us to accomplish His work. He makes that very obvious."

She was, however, without sadness: "My sanctity is a failure . . . but He Alone counts." She was haunted by the thought: "God Alone, Alone." "If you only knew, when one has been on the brink of death, how empty-handed one feels—a poor nothing before the infinity of God!"

"*May every call of Your grace, every manifestation of Your Will, all the circumstances of my life, all its deceptions, pains or sufferings, even the call of death itself, find me in this attitude: willing, offered, offering with You, by You, in You.*"

Mother Elisabeth on her sick bed.

She confided:

"This state of humiliation, I think, comes from an interior grace to establish me in the truth. Moments of deep union with Jesus have always had this characteristic of barrenness where I would lose myself and disappear in Infinite Immensity, in infinite grandeur, near to which I become always more 'nothing'."

In her prayer, she now used only "His" words—those of Jesus:

Ad Patrem . . . Per Ipsum.

"Here am I, O Father.

Father, I thank You for having heard my prayer. I know that You always hear Me.

Father, save Me from this hour. But it is for this hour that I have come.

Father, glorify Thy Name.

I praise Thee, Father, Lord of heaven and earth, for having hidden these things from the wise and prudent and revealed them to little ones. Yes Father, for such was Thy good pleasure.

Father, glorify Thy Son, that Thy Son may glorify Thee.

Now, O Father, glorify Me with Thyself, with the glory which I had with Thee before the world began.

Righteous Father, keep them in Thy Name, those whom Thou hast given Me.

Father, Thou in Me and I in them, that they may be one in Us.

Father, I will that there where I am they also may be, that they may see the glory Thou hast given Me, because Thou hast loved Me before the creation of the world.

Righteous Father, the world has not known Thee,

but I have known Thee.

Father, forgive them.

Father, if it be possible, let this cup . . .

Father, into Thy hands I commend my spirit . . .

Father, I have glorified Thee on earth . . . I have finished the work Thou gavest Me to do."

☐

In the novitiate, everyone was praying fervently for the cure of Mother Elisabeth. For a moment. their prayers seemed to be answered: she was advised to take up a little activity. From her bed. she gave her novices a few lessons.

It cost her to bow to this manifestation of God's Will: "I was all ready to go to heaven, and Mother General told me I still have to keep living. Well then, I want it too . . . I'm going to get back to my task."

According to her own expression, she felt "finished". Then, always there was that desire tormenting her, because it was the expression of the firm will of her Master for her: to be identified with Him. To be so in reality, in solitude, since her Master had suffered alone.

"It seems to me that I see written on the above curtains these words in large letters, 'Alone, I was Alone.' I am too well cared for. But you'll see. I shall die alone."

She was teased about her "peopled solitude". During the day, visits hardly ever ceased, and during the night her Little Sister nurse slept in her room. She insisted: "You'll see, if He has taken me seriously, I shall die alone."

Two graces, very special, very powerful, very

significant in their form, made a strong impression on her. Divine touches, followed closely by desolation . . . fear, dread, terror of possible illusion.

"It's not just anything to be identified . . . I asked for it "no matter what the cost'. He is taking me seriously, but it's not just anything! . . . I didn't know all I was asking for—it is terrible to our poor nature."

On the eve of the feast of Christ the King, Mother Elisabeth sent an invitation to the novitiate:

"My 'good evening' is a little early since you are still gathering turnips, and I am taking advantage of a moment of solitude to send this to you. It will get to you more surely.

First of all, I want to say that I shall 'see you tomorrow'. The 'quarters' will be ready to receive you all. . . . Together we shall sing about the beautiful kingdom of Jesus, the kingdom where each one of us has her place, where each one contributes to its Beauty, to its Glory, and should add her personal note of love and holiness."

For the first time since she had been in the infirmary, she wanted to preside at recreation. When it was time, the Sisters went to get her and Mother Elisabeth recommended: "Stay close to me, because I am not yet too steady." But she had hardly sat down in the midst of "her World" than she became so full of life and gaiety that she almost gave the illusion of being cured.

That year, the feast of All Saints fell the day after the solemnity of Christ the King. During three days in succession there was High Mass and sung Vespers. Although she had a slight cold, she assisted at the ceremonies and, as on every feast, the liturgy gave her immense joy.

After High Mass on November 2nd, she was at the end of her strength. Her sister helped her back to bed, dismayed to know she was feeling so badly. She reassured her, "This slight cold is nothing . . . I ask your pardon for giving you so much trouble!"

Once back in bed again, and calm, she looked at her "little sister": "My Little Sister Marie-Thérèse, how quickly our life has passed!"

During the day, she spoke of what could give someone consolation in their last moments, and she appeared to be in anguish. Suddenly her gaze rested on a statue representing Our Lady under a title she loved most, "Sedes Sapientiae", and her face lit up. "When you think that she will be there to welcome us. Our Blessed Mother—all I have received from her will never be known . . ."

A note to the novices, the last one, was dated that November 2nd. Her fine, pointed handwriting which, twenty-five years beforehand had enthusiastically annotated the book "Paroles d'un Revenant", betrayed a weary hand that evening, but the style held the youthfulness of a soul carried away by an immense enthusiasm:

". . . in reflecting about time, which passes and which is so swiftly spent, I thought of the beautiful words of Cardinal Mercier. . . . 'In heaven my love will no longer increase, nor my glory nor, especially, that which I could have rendered to Christ, to God. Oh! How precious time is!'

Consider the value of time in this way and, each night, instead of regretting all the small, insignificant things in which the will played such a small part, regret rather that which could have given glory to Our Lord by a smiling, generous acceptation of His Will and which you have perhaps let pass you by . . ."

On Wednesday the 3rd, Mother Elisabeth's infirmarian preferred to forbid her receiving the novices until her cold was better. A simple precaution, to prevent more fatigue — a matter of several days, at most.

On Thursday, troubled by learning that a novice had just received news of the death of a friend in painful circumstances, Mother Elisabeth could not bring herself to wait several days, and delegated one of her Aides to console the novice in her place.

On the following day, the First Friday of the month, she sent the novitiate their "order of the day": the Gloria Patri.

□

Nothing particular happened during the afternoon. A few minutes before six-thirty, one of her assistants, passing by the room, went in. Mother Elisabeth was the first to speak: "Good evening, Sister."

"Good evening, Mother."

The "poor human word which begins and ends everything" seemed powerless to open a conversation. Mother Elisabeth's countenance reflected profound suffering. Three times the same greeting was exchanged, then in an anguished tone of voice she added, simply: "Pray for me." And the door closed on the solitude of her soul.

One day, she had written:

"Jesus, alone in the face of anguish and death— nothing from earth, nothing from the Father! To expect nothing, to ask nothing from this earth in my hours of anguish, to console Your isolation. To accept the silence of the Father, Your Father, O Jesus! My God, I accept the death You have prepared for me, uniting it with Yours. May it be the supreme hommage of my adoration and my love! I love it, I accept in advance this separation as the last gift of my free and voluntary love."

"Death," she used to say, "is the next to last step in our conformity to Our Lord."

"Behold the Bridegroom is coming: such must be for me the utterance, the cry of death's approach. May this cry echo in a soul by then detached, purified, sanctified, in a soul filled with the one desire of God Alone.

It is time for us to see each other, O my Beloved Lord."

☐

As dawn broke on November 5th, 1948, the Lord had passed by. Mother Elisabeth no longer belonged to this earth.

■

Appendices

✝ *"Father, all I ask, my one desire, is to have within me the sentiments of Christ Jesus, Your Son and my God."*

The Way of the Cross

Father, all I ask, my one desire, is "to have within me the sentiments of Christ Jesus," Your Son and my God.

May Your Spirit assist me in this moment, to adhere to all the movements of His Holy Soul during His Sorrowful Passion, so that I, His Spouse, Your Child, may share His "Sorrow for sin," seeking out the slightest traces of it in my life. And may I enter at last, with full generosity, into that spirit of reparation to which your Grace is calling me.

Mary, Mother of Sorrows, Virgo Reparatrix, receive, enlighten, guide the soul of your child, you who "know" Jesus.

✝ **I** . Jesus is condemned to death.

Jesus, silent before the High Priest—the crowd full of hatred—He makes no reply; He accepts—His condemnation is merited: "He was made sin for my sake."

In Him, I am condemned: enter into His Silence, into the Truth and the Love of His Silence—apply to myself the grace of this loving and silent acceptation—allow myself to be judged; allow myself to be bared; keep silent.

✝ **II** The Body of Jesus, exhausted, aching, the flesh torn by the scourging. . . . The heavy Cross makes Him quiver with intense pain, the Features of His Divine Face are drawn with agony.

It is the weight of the Cross—I should not be astonished to feel it, at times to be crushed by it.

Jesus trembles; He accepts.

The Cross is the nourishment and the means of Love.

✝ **III** Contemplate the powerlessness of Jesus who weakens, stumbles, falls.

Adore this powerlessness willed by the Almighty Divinity.

Abase myself before this weakness of the "Divine

Strength"—be astonished at so much love, at a love truly "real".

My God, Jesus, I no longer complain about my limitations of all kinds: I want them; I love them.

O powerless God!

✝ **IV** Mary, your Sorrow—I am the cause of it. Help your child to understand this.

You understand the Divine Heart! Your Sorrow is immense, calm—nothing of yourself. You are suffering for Him, you are sharing, accepting. Teach me.

✝ **V** Jesus, God, helped, sustained by His creature. Jesus, You seem to be "Incapable" by Yourself.

Be the Divine Remedy which heals my pride, my need to be and to do.

Would that I could help You, carry part of Your Cross by discreetly helping others to carry theirs— by accepting Your Offer when you pass.

✝ **VI** Face of Jesus—"He is without splendour, without beauty. There is nothing to attract attention. We saw Him and did not recognise Him."

Face of Jesus, Face veiled and as though disfigured by my sin—Hide me in the "secret of Your Face: may I there at last learn this difficult thing: to love to be hidden, unknown, forgotten, to count for nothing.

✝ **VII** Jesus falls a second time: He is weakening, exhausted, faltering—reality of a love that is true, of that Unique Love who has given all of Himself, even the joy of feeling that He is giving.

The grace to love, within the feeling of my own wretchedness and of my powerlessness, together with that feeling, even when I have nothing else to offer.

✝ **VIII** Jesus overburdened, consoles others.

Jesus-God, You alone could be so kind, so unselfish.

Jesus, teach me how to forget myself, to keep silent, to hide my own suffering, to console You in consoling others.

Jesus, as for myself, let me be consoled by You alone.

✝ **IX** The summit of Calvary.

The excessive pain, the overwhelming distress . . . the poor Body sags, and Jesus falls once more.

"It was not for fun that He loved me."

Jesus, powerless, I adore You in your very powerlessness.

I love my own: powerlessness in prayer, powerlessness to be virtuous, powerlessness to love.

X Jesus is stripped.

Stripping that is painful, humiliating.

Contemplate Him in silence, ask Him to apply this stripping to my soul: the grace of "Nakedness," condition of intimate union with Him.

"Follow in nakedness, Jesus Christ naked." (Imitation)

Jesus, take everything from me, but be Jesus for me.

XI Jesus, nailed to the Cross — fastened, immobile—

Immobile in Love, in the Will of the Father.

Jesus, the grace of this "Immobility" in times of trial which are not disturbed by any desire, any regret, any turning back.

Fastened in love.

XII Mysterious abandonment.

Isolation of the Holy Soul of my Master. "My God, why have You abandoned me?"

Isolation: Jesus alone in face of anguish and of

death: nothing from earth, nothing from the Father.

To expect nothing; to ask for nothing from this earth during my hours of anguish; to console Your Isolation. To accept the Silence of the Father, and Your own, O Jesus.

My God, I accept the death You have prepared for me, uniting it with Yours. May it be the supreme hommage of my adoration and my love.

I love, I accept in advance this separation as the last gift of my free and voluntary love.

✝ **XIII** On my knees, near my Sorrowful Mother.

With her, to contemplate the Divine Countenance, the lifeless Body, seeing there the wounds, the marks of His Infinite Love, the assurance of my pardon.

With Mary, enter respectfully into the wound of the pierced Heart, to probe the depth of this Love, to respond to it.

✝ **XIV** The new Sepulchre . . .

That is how my poor soul would like to be tomorrow morning: empty, silent, closed to creatures, all prepared and open for Jesus Alone.

Then, by the Holy Species, beneath their Veil, you Mary will place the Body of your Divine Son in this soul which wants to be poor, detached, uniquely ambitious for its God.

PASSION OF JESUS, strengthen me.

Counsels and Notes

Counsels:

We must believe, believe blindly in the love of Our Lord and in His plans for us, continuing to believe even when confronted by adverse circumstances, even by the Cross. Our very weaknesses should not make us doubt: He is All Powerful and He loves us. MARCH 1945

☐

When you will have learned this science of sciences: "living with God", you will have learned everything.

☐

May the thought of your interior sanctuary sustain you, help you to live within, even whilst giving yourself generously to exterior tasks. This thought alone: God is within me, He is my Guest, should suffice to orient and sustain a whole lifetime.

☐

Be a soul of deep faith, a soul fully supernatural, keeping your eyes fixed on your "purpose" and making use of everything to unite yourself more closely to Our Lord.

□

Love prayer. May your soul be always orientated towards prayer. What is important in prayer is to come very close to Our Lord by faith, to communicate with the dispositions of His Heart — humility, generosity, love.   MARCH 1944

□

The best prayer is that which leaves us more humble, more determined to forget ourselves, to put ourselves aside, to accept sacrifice.

□

Love everything which makes us disappear, everything that is humble and lowly. Our devotedness should be loyal, hidden, without show, without any natural self-seeking.

□

It is God's Will which sanctifies us. Let us ask our Blessed Lady to teach us that. She who desired that all should be done according to this Will. Look at Mary as a child, so little, so motionless in her small crib, and try to be as little and as motionless in God's Hands.

□

Let us remain hidden in the Heart of the Most Blessed Virgin, until she shows Jesus to us in His full light, on the day of Eternity.

Notes:

Prayer is, above all, a meeting, a contact with God.

The important condition, the "pre-supposition" for prayer, is the "freedom" of soul which must be brought to it.

The only, the main obstacle to prayer, to intimate closeness to God, is attachment to things created, being occupied with self, or some good thing loved inordinately.

Prayer, then, "pre-supposes" the "interior liturgy", that is to say, the interior ordering of our movements, the hierarchy of our faculties. All that is the result of despoliation, of detachment, of the liberation of the soul.

How to pray:

—pray with courage: that is to say, to persist, to persevere in prayer despite aridity, desolation, difficulties;

—pray also in a "supernatural way", with the dispositions of Jesus, pray in Jesus.

He is the Only Son of the Father: pray with Him, in Him, as a Child of the Father.

He is the Saviour: pray for all souls—to bring to our prayer the entire world, which Jesus carried in His prayer.

□

Jesus is Everything.

He is the Great "Simplifier" of our spiritual life.

He sums up everything. He is the "synthesis" of the human and the divine.

Love Him and follow Him enthusiastically because He is "Himself".

He is the Splendour of the Father, the Splendour of Humanity.

The Prologue of Saint John's Gospel expresses what He is as God:

Equal to the Father.

The Splendour of the Father.

Splendour of Humanity: He is supremely "wondrous" and "divinely good".

Above all else, we must cling to this Adorable Person of Our Lord: the "All" of our religious life.

Love Him for this divine Splendour and this human perfection "united" in Him.

Love Him also because of His exigencies.

He asks for everything and He exacts everything.

Love Him because He asks for everything.

☐

Jesus, my Model of Sanctity, Model given me by the Father, I should be "famished for holiness" for Your sake.

Anyone who has glimpsed "Your value", O my God, how can she falter in her love?

Keep this desire alive in me, this hunger for You. Make it sincere, O Jesus, and grant that my life be fervent and my soul active in seeking everything You will, so as to accomplish it through love.

☐

O Jesus, "the Father's first Religious", at Mass I love to penetrate Your attitude of oblation. I try to unite myself with it, to "conform" to it my own "poor weak oblation".

O Jesus, identify my soul with this "movement" of your Holy Soul. May I be, so to say, affixed in this attitude of offering which is so very much Your own.

May every call of Your grace, every manifestation of Your Will, all the circumstances of my life, all its deceptions, pains or sufferings, even the call of death itself, find me in this attitude: willing, offered, offering with You, by You, in You.

Lord my God, today and henceforth, I willingly accept, and with all my heart, the kind of death, the kind of life it will please you to send me, with all its pains, all its suffering and all its anguish.

O Jesus, receive me from the hands of the Most Blessed Virgin. Offer me, immolate me together with Yourself. I offer myself to You through her and I unite myself to Your incessant Immolation so that You may be pleased, through me, with me and in me, to satisfy your burning desire to work still for the glory of Your Father and for the salvation of souls, particularly for the perfection of Your Priests and of chosen souls.

"Through her, with her, in her."

Concerning her, concerning my Mother, how can I tell of her greatness? Mother of God, Mother of the Word, Covenant of the Blessed Trinity—all these privileges prepare or crown her Divine Maternity: Magnificat.

She is my Mother: my life, everything worthwhile, everything good received has come to me through her.

My Model: perfectly "identified" with all the movements of Jesus' Soul.

My Mistress: She is there, the Throne of Wisdom, who enlightens me, guides me, instructs me, restores me.

My Mediatrix: her "Mediation" consists above all in a work of union between Mary and the soul. "Hidden in the womb of Mary, I shall there be protected, nourished, given growth by this dear Mother until she gives me birth in Glory."

Then will she be for me "Janua Caeli" and will give me forever to Jesus, her Divine Son.

She has already given Him to me:

Ever since you, most Holy Virgin, have entered more fully, more truly into my life, Jesus, your Son and my God, is also there more fully.

Come, enter it even more fully and, through you and with you, Jesus will come and will invade my poor soul.

■

— NOTES —